Potomac Appalachian Trail Club

Cabins

2016 Edition

A guide to cabins maintained by and available for rent from the Potomac Appalachian Trail Club

Potomac Appalachian Trail Club
118 Park Street, SE
Vienna, VA 22180-4609
703-242-0315
www.patc.net

Potomac Appalachian Trail Club Cabins
2016 Edition

Edited by
Anstr Davidson
Alan Kahan

Copyright © 2016 by Potomac Appalachian Trail Club
All rights reserved.

Published by Potomac Appalachian Trail Club
118 Park Street, SE
Vienna, VA 22180-4609
www.patc.net

Library of Congress Control Number: 2016949811
ISBN 978-0-915746-71-2

All rights reserved. No part of this book may be used or reproduced in any manner whatsoever without written permission except for brief quotations in reviews and articles.

The Potomac Appalachian Trail Club (PATC) is a volunteer-supported 501(c)(3) non-profit formed in 1927 for the purpose of building and maintaining the Appalachian Trail (AT), a 2,190-mile footpath from Maine to Georgia, the longest hiking-only trail in the world.

We are the trail guardians for over 1,000 miles of trails in Pennsylvania, Maryland, West Virginia, Virginia, and the District of Columbia, including 240 miles of AT. Our territory begins in Central Pennsylvania at Pine Grove Furnace, continues through Maryland and West Virginia to Harpers Ferry and extends into the mid-point of Virginia, including Shenandoah National Park. In addition, we maintain more than 800 miles of other regional trails, 1,000 acres of land, and more than 80 shelters and cabins.

CONTENTS

About this Book 5
Overview 5
What the Renter Needs to Know Before Going 6
Planning a Trip 7
At the Cabin 9
Leaving the Cabin 14
How to Rent a Cabin 15
Other Options 15
Rules 15
Sources for Information and Assistance 16
Land Stewardship 16
Vining Tract History 17
Cabin Location Map 18
PATC Cabins At-a-Glance 20

Cabins in Pennsylvania
Silberman Trail Center (*Member-only*) 22
Anna Michener Cabin 24
Milesburn Cabin 26
Gypsy Spring Cabin (*Member-only*) 28
Little Cove Cabin (*Member-only*) 30
The Hermitage Cabin 32
Dawson Cabin 34

Cabins in Maryland
Little Orleans Cabin (*Member-only*) 36
Catoctin Hollow Lodge 38
Olive Green Cabin 40
Bear Spring Cabin 42

Cabins in West Virginia/Northern Virginia
Highacre House (*Member-only*) 44
Blackburn Trail Center (*Member-only*) 46
Bears Den Cottage Cabin 48
Myron Glaser Cabin (*Member-only*) 50
Sugar Knob Cabin 52
Glass House Cabin (*Member-only*) 54
Horwitz Cabin (*Member-only*) 56

Cabins in and near Shenandoah National Park, Virginia
Range View Cabin 58
Lambert Cabin (*Member-only*) 60
Tulip Tree Cabin (*Member-only*) 62
Huntley Cabin (*Member-only*) 64
Corbin Cabin 66
Old Rag Cabin (*Member-only*) 68
Rock Spring Cabin 70

Meadows Cabin (*Member-only*) 72
Cliff's House Cabin (*Member-only*) 74
Robert Humphrey Cabin (*Member-only*) 76
Jones Mountain Cabin 78
Pocosin Cabin 80
Rosser Lamb Cabin (*Member-only*) 82
John's Rest Cabin (*Member-only*) 84
Argow Cabin (*Member-only*) 86
J. Frank Schairer Trail Center (*Member-only*) 88
Doyles River Cabin 90

The Vining Tract Cabins, Virginia
Mutton Top Cabin (*Member-only*) 92
Morris Cabin (*Member-only*) 94
Johnson Cabin 96
Wineberry Cabin (*Member-only*) 98
Conley Cabin (*Member-only*) 100
Vining Cabin (*Member-only*) 102

Cabins In Charlottesville, Virginia
Dunlodge (*Member-only*) 104

Other Accommodations
Bears Den Lodge and Hostel 106

PATC Cabins Summary 107
Acknowledgements 108

From its elevation of about 2,800 feet, the Doyles River Cabin, in the South District of Shenandoah National Park, overlooks a picturesque valley with views of Cedar Mountain and Via Gap.

ABOUT THIS BOOK

This book describes PATC's cabins in detail—their layouts, locations, and features. The cabins are ordered geographically in the book going from north (southern Pennsylvania) to south (Charlottesville, Virginia). The book is designed to describe the cabin experience to first-time renters, as well as help experienced cabin renters choose new cabins to explore.

This edition of the book includes floor plans. Volunteers visited each cabin to create the plans so that the reader will have a better idea of where the bunks, stoves, and other important items are. These plans are supplemented by interior photographs. When viewing the plans and photos, remember that items like chairs and tables move.

This book does not describe the cabin rental process itself. That process is described on the cabin website, www.patc.net/cabins, where the rates and rules are set out, and where one can reserve a cabin. There are important rules that apply to the processes of renting and using a cabin. Some are referred to in this book, but all rules are listed officially on the website.

This book also explains why renting a cabin may not be the right thing for everyone. There are risks to renting a cabin. Most are set out here.

Overall, we hope this book will enhance the experience at a PATC cabin.

OVERVIEW

PATC cabins have several origins. Initially, the club built cabins to house trail work parties in areas beyond easy commuting distance from Washington, DC. Other cabins were built by forest rangers or the Civilian Conversation Corps for recreation, by early settlers for homes, or by those seeking retreats away from the city. Many cabins were donated to PATC. Now these structures provide shelter for those who want to escape urban living, experience the way our forebearers lived, and explore the woods and mountains with less effort and more amenities than backpacking (but with more isolation than at a public campground).

The cabins range from one-room structures with no indoor plumbing or electricity to houses with modern amenities.

Cabins are located from southern Pennsylvania south to Charlottesville, Virginia. Most are on or near the Blue Ridge Mountains and the Appalachian Trail (AT). A few are further west. All require at least an hour drive from Washington, DC, and many also require a hike from the nearest parking.

The cabins range from one-room structures with no indoor plumbing or electricity to houses with modern amenities. We refer to the former as "primitive cabins" and the latter as "modern." There are a few in the middle—"semi-primitive"—that, for example, have electricity but no indoor plumbing.

Three cabins are designated as "trail centers." This means that their initial purpose was to support trail use or maintenance. They tend to be larger than other cabins, and are more often unavailable for general rental because of use by trail work crews or long-distance hikers. When available, they may be rented like any other cabin.

No two cabins are exactly alike. Each has individual features that set it apart from the others and make it a favorite for a loyal group of renters.

Exploring new cabins is part of the charm of the cabin experience.

All the cabins are maintained by unpaid PATC members. Both routine maintenance and major repairs are accomplished with volunteer labor. Only rarely will a paid contractor work at a cabin. Volunteers also staff the cabins desk to help club members and the public with the cabin rental process.

New cabins occasionally are added to the club's inventory and, rarely, does a cabin leave the inventory. While this book is accurate as of its date of publication, prospective renters should consult the cabins website, www.patc.net/cabins, for updated information.

WHAT THE RENTER NEEDS TO KNOW BEFORE GOING

A trip to a PATC cabin can be a wonderful experience. These cabins are historic ties to a simpler, but harder way of life. For many, the simplicity and challenge of living at these cabins is part of their charm, but a prospective renter needs to know the challenges. These cabins are not hotels, and they are not for everyone. They are an outdoors experience.

A prospective renter should know the following about PATC cabins. Most of these factors apply to all cabins, though not always equally.

> **Staying at a PATC cabin will involve a simpler but harder way of life and is not for everyone.**

- **There is no maid service; there is no trash service.** The renter must clean up and prepare the cabin for the next renter. This means washing dishes, sweeping, mopping, picking up, and so forth. Trash must be hauled back out as well. No one else will do it.
- **Opening and closing the cabin takes time.** These cabins are in remote locations. They are locked and many are shuttered for their protection. It can take time to unlock, open the shutters, and otherwise prepare the cabin for use. It also takes time to close everything upon departure. A portion of a renter's time at a cabin will be taken up with this process.
- **The cabins are in the woods.** Cabins can go several days without renters. Mice, rats, ticks, mosquitoes, bees, wasps, deer, bears, snakes, and other animals can be found in or around the cabin. Snakes may be a particular worry for some renters, but they are beneficial around the cabins since they help control the rodent population and are not aggressive if not molested. Those who fear snakes should not rent a cabin. Renters are not allowed to harm or kill snakes.
- **Cabins can be hard to get to.** Many cabins require a hike in. All require a drive to the trailhead or the cabin itself. The drive often includes rural, unimproved roads. The hike in can be arduous.
- **They are hard to heat.** Most cabins, even the modern ones, depend on firewood for heat. The renter must gather and cut the wood. This takes time and effort. In cold weather, cabins can take a great deal of work to heat. Some cannot be heated well in extremely cold weather.
- **Water may not be drinkable.** The water at most primitive cabins comes from ground water sources such as a nearby river or spring and must be purified. Springs can be seasonal. *Check the cabin listing to determine whether you will need to carry in or purify water.*
- **Toilets.** Most bathrooms are outside and don't flush. They don't smell like the toilet at home.
- **Old stuff.** Renters should not expect modern conveniences. Pots,

pans, utensils, and stoves may be old.
- **Broken stuff.** Things can break at a cabin, and there is no one but the renter to deal with it.
- **Safety.** Stairs, railings, bunks, and porches can be steep or out of alignment. Care must be used.
- **Risks for small children.** Most cabins contain many risks for small children—hot stoves, bunks to fall out of, porches to fall off of, and sharp saws. A renter should consider carefully before taking a child to a cabin. If you bring a child, you must supervise that child closely.
- **They are far from civilization.** For most cabins, it's a long way to a store or emergency help. There is often no cell phone access.
- **Weather.** A cabin trip is very dependent upon the weather for its enjoyment.
- **Maintenance.** Occasionally, the club will have to perform required maintenance during a renter's visit, such as repairs or mowing. The club tries to minimize maintenance-related intrusions, but that is not always possible.
- **Hunting.** In late fall, hunting may occur on property near some of the cabins, so consider wearing blaze orange clothing as a safety precaution when hiking in the area.

Many renters consider the above factors to be features of the cabin experience, but the renter assumes real risks. PATC cannot control these risks and they are not cause for a refund.

PLANNING A TRIP

Getting there

This book describes the conditions one should expect—such as unmaintained roads, steep hills—on the journey to the cabin, but does not provide specific driving directions. Renters will receive directions and GPS coordinates after they make the cabin rental. A GPS device is very helpful and highly recommended.

The directions usually describe a route from the Washington, DC area to parking for the cabin. Those coming from elsewhere need to consult a map to modify the directions for their circumstances.

The trip will usually involve rural roads. Most are improved and state-maintained. There is often, however, a portion of the trip on unimproved roads. While a four-wheel drive vehicle is rarely required, a car may need good ground clearance. The length of the hike from parking lot to cabin varies, and may be impacted by weather conditions.

Renters can drive right up to some cabins in good conditions, but front door parking is not guaranteed for any cabin. Many cabins have alternative parking and longer hike-ins for bad weather. It is wiser to park and walk than to get stuck or damage a car. Consider the impact on your vehicle and the property if proceeding seems hazardous.

After a cabin rental is made, renters will receive a Cabin Direction Sheet with GPS coordinates and other cabin information details.

What to bring

While individual cabins will have slightly different requirements, the same items should be taken to most cabins. Experienced renters have their own packing lists. Below are suggestions on how to make your own.

Certain items should be at the cabin, but if in doubt, bring a spare. You can leave it in your car if not needed.

PLEASE CARRY OUT ANYTHING YOU BRING IN!

Items to bring by group:

- **Heat**
  - *Matches.* Bring a full box. Keep them dry!
  - *Gloves* (preferably those designed to work with hot items). Working with the fire and wood will be dirty. Some cabins have gloves, some do not.
  - *The newspaper.* It may be needed to start the fire. Renters without experience starting fires also may want to bring yesterday's paper.
  - *Handsaw.* There should be one there, but if not, that is a big problem. Renters should have a saw in their cars. A saw is also handy if there is a downed tree across the road.
- **Water**
  - *Bring a gallon.* It may be needed before the ground water can be purified.
  - *Water filter, if this option is used for purification.* In the winter, boiling may be better since there will be a hot fire anyway, and cooling the water after boiling will be easier.
- **Light**
  - *Candles and/or lanterns.* Don't underestimate how dark it will be inside the cabin.
  - *Flashlight.* An outside toilet is usually unlit. Renters may arrive at night. Portable light is necessary.
  - *Headlamp.* Points light where the wearer is looking.
  - *Extra batteries.* (If there are dead batteries in the cabin, please pack them out.)
- **Cooking**
  - *Small gas stove* (i.e., for backpacking). The wood cooking stove takes a great deal of effort to start and produces unwanted heat in the summer. A camping stove does a much better job in making the morning's coffee.
  - *Coffee pot.* The only cooking pot that should be needed. Most cabins have a coffee pot, but it has usually seen much better days. A decent coffee pot is a luxury many will want; and filters!
  - *Can opener/bottle opener/corkscrew.* There will be something there, but it may be old. If you bring a can opener or anything else to the cabin, be sure to take it with you when you leave.
  - *Cool storage.* Renters will want to keep food cool, especially in the summer. Be sure to carry out any coolers you bring in.
- **Sleeping**
  - *Sleeping bags, blankets, and sheets.* Renters will receive a Cabin Direction Sheet that describes the sleeping arrangements. For primitive and semi-primitive cabins, most renters will want to bring a sleeping bag or, in warmer months, a sheet. Renters should bring sheets to modern cabins. Many cabins have blankets, but often not enough for all occupants. Blankets are often musty or worse. Some cabins have no blankets.

- *Pillows.* Renters should bring pillows and pillow cases.
- **Sundries**
  - *Dish towels*
  - *Paper towels*
  - *Salt, pepper, butter, grease, etc.*
  - *Soap, for dishes and the body*
  - *Toilet paper*
  - *Plastic trash bags*
  - *Bath towel*
- **Personal**
  - *Toiletries*
  - *Bug spray*
  - *Camp shoes*
  - *Sunscreen*
- **Miscellaneous**
  - *Alarm clock*
  - *Radio*
  - *Games.* There will be games there, but the deed for Park Place may be missing.
  - *Sun shower.* It will be wonderful in the summer. In the winter, it can be used to carry water.
- **Food**
  - *Renter's call, of course.* The further the hike in, the more important that it's light backpacking food.
  - *Cans, not bottles.*
  - *Frozen food can double as ice until it melts.*
  - *Remember, everything not consumed must be packed out!*
- **First aid**
  - *First aid kit with medicines the renter needs*

The list of things to bring can get lengthy, so use your judgement in making your own list based on the cabin at which you are staying.

Each renter needs to make his or her own list from the above. It will vary by cabin.

How does one carry this all in? For short hike-ins, it may be easier to make multiple trips with reusable grocery bags. But that will get old if the hike-in is long. In that case, a good backpack is best.

Weather

Weather will have a big impact on the trip to the cabin and the enjoyment of the time there. Weather is part of the challenge. Renters should pack to be prepared for different kinds of weather. Bad weather may also lead to spending time on indoor activities at the cabin instead of hiking or exploring around it.

AT THE CABIN

Heat—wood and stoves

Most cabins, even modern ones, rely on firewood for heat. In cold weather, keeping the cabin warm can take considerable time and effort. The renter must gather and cut the wood.

Most cabins, even modern ones, rely on firewood for heat so the renter must gather and cut the wood. In cold weather, keeping the cabin warm can take considerable time and effort.

Gathering wood

Cabins that use wood heat have wood sources nearby in fallen limbs and blowdowns. Only down and dead timber may be collected; it is prohibited to cut or use anything that is standing or live. Renters should not bring wood from elsewhere due to issues with invasive species. Wood is to be collected only from the cabin property. The Cabin Direction Sheet and instructions for renters at the cabin will include information, and often a map, describing where wood may be collected. Available wood may be relatively far from the cabin.

Cutting wood

The cabin should have a bow saw and a splitting maul. There will also be a place to cut and split the wood—usually a sawhorse and chopping block. Do not cut or split wood inside the cabin or on decks, porches, rocks, or concrete.

Saws can break. It is a good idea to have a backup saw in the car in case the cabin's saw is broken.

Burning wood

Cabins have various places to burn wood for heat. These are:

- **Fireplaces**—use more wood than a stove, but give off more light than a stove. However, a fireplace will not heat a cabin.
- **Fireplace inserts**—metal boxes inside a traditional fireplace. Fireplace inserts work like stoves. They are more efficient than a fireplace. Those in cabins with electricity often have fans to circulate the warm air into the room.

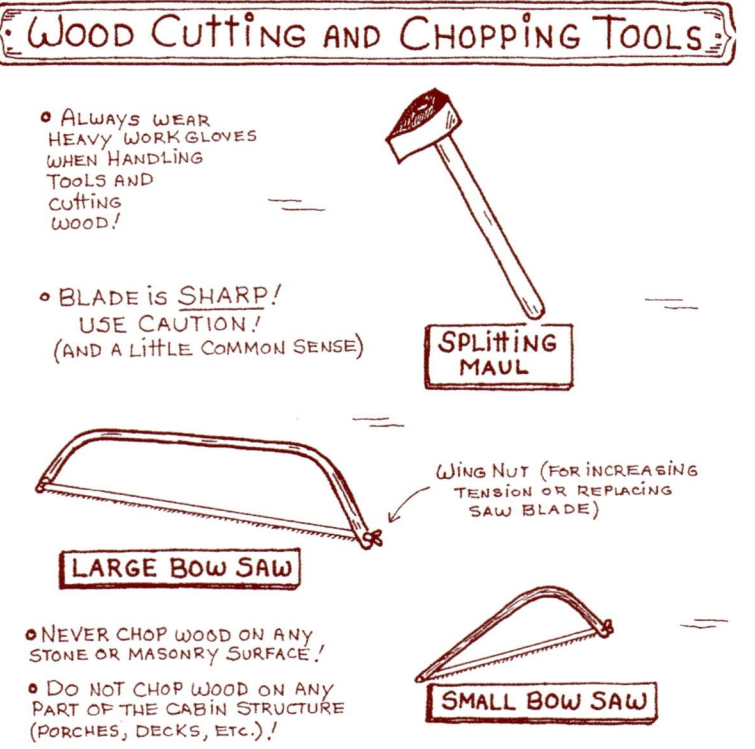

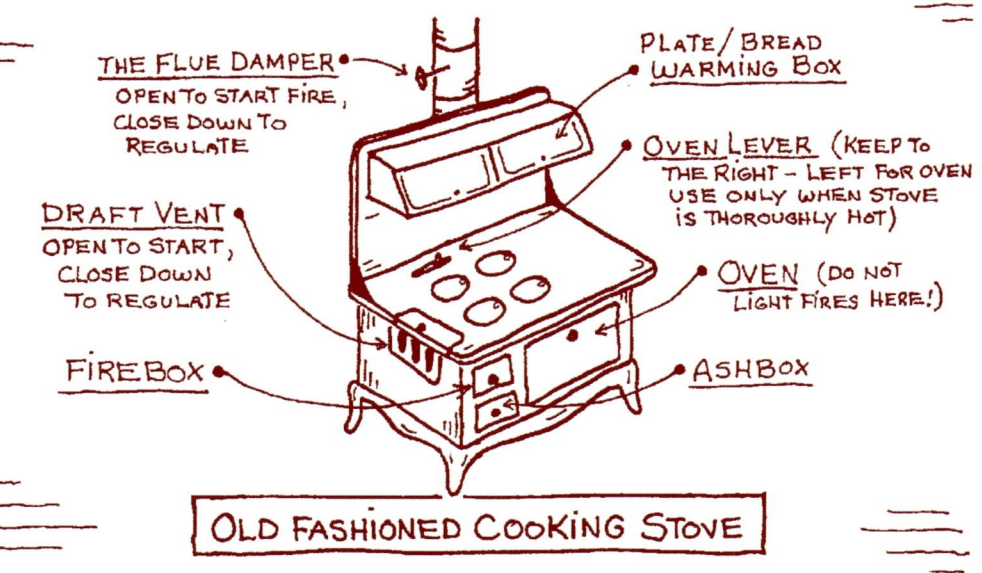

- **Heating stoves**—metal or ceramic containers for burning wood. They are more efficient than a fireplace and use less wood. There are various shapes, sizes, and kinds of stoves at the cabins. See below for tips on using a stove.
- **Heating stoves that can also heat water or food**—these have flat tops and often disks to put pots on. Anything placed on a stove needs to be watched carefully since spills may cause damage. These stoves are designed primarily for heat, not cooking. Don't light one just to boil water if the heat is not needed!
- **Wood cooking stoves**—designed to cook food, not to heat the room. They provide some heat but not enough to keep the cabin comfortable on a cold night. These stoves will, however, produce enough heat to be very uncomfortable to use in warm weather.

Even the most efficient stove may have difficulty keeping the cabin warm in extremely cold weather.

POTOMAC APPALACHIAN TRAIL CLUB CABINS 11

Tips on wood stoves
- Stoves are meant for wood, not coal or charcoal. Treat stoves with care.
- Examine the stove. Read the instructions provided in the cabin manual, if any. Find the flue, ash drawer, firebox, and air vents. Also, look for an insulated glove to wear while working around the hot stove.
- Empty the ash drawer. Put the ashes in the ash bucket and take them outside to the ash pit. If the ash pit is full, spread cooled ashes in the woods.
- Open the flue damper (handle parallel to air flow), if there is one. Open all vents and the door.
- Build a starter pile of paper, twigs, wood chips (collect them near the chopping block). Do not use any liquid (e.g., charcoal lighter fluid) to start the fire.
- Have progressively larger dry wood handy. Light the starter fire. After the starter fire ignites, add wood carefully.
- When the fire is established, reduce the air flow through the vents and close the door. Leave the flue open! Change air flow to adjust heat produced and rate of burn. Add wood through the door.

Leaving cut wood for the next renter
Cabin renters must leave enough cut wood for the next renter's first night or as much as was there when the renter arrived—whichever is greater. Cut the wood short enough to fit in the fireplace or stove. Be sure some of the wood is dry—in wet weather, try to burn damp wood once the fire is going well and save the dry to start the next fire. Also, leave dry twigs and small branches.

Allow the fire to die out completely before leaving. *Do not use water on a fire in a wood stove or fireplace!*

Water—springs and streams
Primitive cabins rely on nearby ground water—springs or streams. Modern cabins usually have well water.

Springs and streams vary considerably in their flow and reliability. Some springs flow well even through dry summer weather; others have a greatly reduced flow or even disappear. Renters should bring some water to any cabin in case there is a problem with the local ground water.

All ground water should be treated—boiling, filtering, or chemical treatment—before consuming.

Before consuming, all ground water should be purified by boiling, filtering, or chemical treatment.

Most cabins have containers to carry water from the source to the cabin. The renter might, however, bring a collapsible container. A sun shower can serve this purpose well.

Cooking—stoves, pots, utensils, plates
The cabins have pots, pans, dishes, silverware, glasses, and so forth. Some items, particularly coffee pots, can be in poor repair. If there is an item that will be critical to cooking plans, the renter may want to bring it from home. Cabins also have can openers and corkscrews, but these can disappear or not work. The renter might want to bring something to open any container that is taken to the cabin.

Several cabins have propane cooking burners. Unlike a wood stove, these can be started and turned off quickly and add far less heat to the room. Renters should bring a small gas stove (as for backpacking) to cabins that don't have propane stoves. Renters will not want to fire up the wood stove just to boil water in warm weather.

Cleaning

There will be brooms, mops, and other items for cleaning the cabin.

The fireplace or stove should have its own broom and ash bucket. Don't use the regular broom for ashes.

The cabin will have a plastic tub to use as a sink. Some will have real sinks that drain to the ground. Don't put food or scraps down the sink. Garbage should be packed out. Only water should be put down the sink or cast into the woods from the dish tub.

Light

Primitive cabins can be very dark. The renter must bring light—lanterns, candles, flashlights. Candle wax should be carefully controlled. In modern cabins with light bulbs, there are usually replacement bulbs if one goes out.

A fireplace can be a good source of light. The fire need not be large. In those cabins with both a wood stove and a fireplace, the renter can heat with the stove and illuminate with a small fire. However, in some cabins, using both at the same time does not work well.

Don't forget a flashlight for going out at night to the bathroom.

Be sure to pack out all used candles and wax.

Toilets

All primitive cabins have outdoor toilets. Most toilets contain deposits in concrete vaults or pits. A few are "moldering" in that deposits are at ground level and decay with the help of air circulation.

Do not put anything in the outdoor toilet other than human waste and toilet paper. Do not put dishwater or garbage in it.

Be prepared for a walk to the toilet. For sanitary and fragrancy reasons, the toilet is located away from the cabin.

For sanitary and fragrancy reasons, the toilet is located away from the cabin. Be prepared for a walk. Since the toilet is used less frequently than the cabin, it will often have spiders, bees, ants, and other creatures. It should have its own broom to address them.

Modern cabins have indoor plumbing, but it is usually on a septic tank. Do not put anything in a toilet besides human waste and toilet paper.

Sleeping—bunks, mattresses, blankets

While some cabins have beds, most have plywood bunks. All cabins with bunks have mattresses. These mattresses are approximately two inches thick. They are stored in a cage to keep the mice away. The sleeping options are described for each cabin later in this book. Those options are:

- *Mattresses on the floor.* The sleeping floor is often in a loft.
- *Mattresses on plywood bunks.* In this book, one "bunk" sleeps one person. A "double-width bunk" bed sleeps two people adjacent to each other. "Double-deck bunks" sleep two people, one over the other. "Double-width, double-deck" bunks sleep four people, two over the other two.
- *Futons.* Couches that fold into a bed that usually sleeps two.

- ***Beds.*** Traditional beds with mattresses. There are single and double beds. They have a cover, but not sheets, blankets, or pillows.

    Many cabins have wool blankets, but not enough for the rated maximum number of guests. Blankets are not guaranteed. Renters should bring sleeping bags or bedding (sheets, blankets, and pillows).

    The floor plans for each cabin shown later in this book give prospective renters an idea of the layout of the sleeping arrangements.

Furniture

Please do not move furniture or rearrange the cabin layout. If there is a special need to do so, please return the furniture to where you found it when you depart.

Tools—saws and mauls

The cabin should have a saw and a splitting maul. Use these items with care.

If there are multiple saws, try them all. Usually, one is better than the other. Be sure that the blade is properly attached and tight.

Renters should wear gloves when working with these tools. Cabins often have gloves, but they can be in poor condition.

Be very careful when swinging the maul. Know where nearby people are. Use the chopping block.

Log book, other books, games, puzzles

Each cabin has a log book in which renters should enter information about the stay—dates, members of the party, weather, and notable occurrences. Please supervise a child's entry in the log book. It should not be used as a coloring book; nor should paper be torn out of the log book. These are archival-quality books.

The log book is not the best place to alert the overseer to problems about the cabin. Do that on the sheet that is returned with the key. If there is something important that the next renter should know, leave a note where he or she can see it upon arrival.

There will be books, games, and puzzles. Some may have missing pieces. Those wanting to play a serious game of cards, should bring their own decks because card decks at the cabin may not be complete.

Extras—radios, microwaves, thermometers, solar showers

Part of the fun of going to a cabin is finding the surprises that the overseer has left for renters. Most have thermometers both indoors and outdoors. Cabins with electricity often have radios and microwaves. At least two cabins have built-in solar showers. These items are not guaranteed, though.

LEAVING THE CABIN

Cleaning up: Renters must clean the cabin, make everything orderly, and leave enough firewood for the next renter. Renters will receive a checklist of items that must be taken care of before leaving. In short, the cabin needs to be cleaned, secured, and locked.

The floor plans shown for each cabin give prospective renters the layout of the sleeping arrangements and furniture.

Leaving firewood: Renters must leave cut wood for the next person. There is no excuse not to do this. It is good to take care of the wood supply early in a cabin stay and not wait until the last minute. In wet weather, be sure to leave as much dry wood as possible.

Leaving anything else: Don't. "Donations" are not welcome. The next renter will not expect a donation. A donation will be at the cabin until someone packs it out. Especially unwelcome are paper products and food, which attract mice.

Reporting (and fixing) damage: There is likely to be wear, tear, and damage at the cabin. Renters should report anything they find on the Cabin Condition Report included in the Cabin Key Packet. For any repairs considered emergencies, like broken water pipes, windows, or porch railings, renters are asked to contact the Volunteer Overseer listed on the Cabin Direction Sheet received with the Cabin Key Packet. Recording damage in the cabin log book is not helpful since the overseer may not see it quickly. Renters are encouraged to fix broken conditions if they have the expertise to do it.

HOW TO RENT A CABIN

Please read about the cabin rental process and rules on the PATC website, www.patc.net/cabins

All cabins must be rented in advance through PATC headquarters. The rental process is described on the PATC Web site, www.patc.net/cabins.

OTHER OPTIONS

PATC cabins are just one way to enjoy a rustic experience in the woods. There are many campgrounds, private cabins, and other accomodations in the area. Those wanting to stay in Shenandoah National Park should consult its website, www.nps.gov/shen. The park has campgrounds, lodges, trail shelters, and camping in the woods, in addition to six PATC cabins.

RULES

This book refers to several rules that guide the rental and use of the cabins. All the rules are set out on the PATC website, www.patc.net/cabins. Those considering the rental of a cabin should read the rules. Here are important general considerations:

- **Rental process:** The process has time limits, minimum stay requirements, and other such rules designed for fairness. These rules are are applied strictly.
- **Refunds:** Weather and other factors create risks for renters. Our rules on refunds put that risk on the renter. Refunds for weather or other adverse conditions are rare.
- **Cleanup:** The renter must do the cabin cleanup.
- **Hunting:** Please refer to the PATC website, www.patc.net/cabins, for the current policy concerning hunting and firearms on PATC property.

SOURCES FOR INFORMATION AND ASSISTANCE

The website: Up-to-date information about the cabins and how to rent them is on the PATC website, www.patc.net/cabins.

PATC Maps: Most cabins are marked on the relevant PATC map noted on each cabin page. Maps may be obtained on the PATC website, at PATC headquarters, or at many outdoor stores in the mid-Atlantic area.

Contact PATC headquarters: Prospective renters may contact the Cabins Desk at 703-242-0315 ext. 102 or e-mail Cabinsdesk@patc.net. Cabins Desk hours normally are Monday through Friday from 11:30 am to 1:30 pm, but check the website to see if there are additional times. (PATC headquarters is closed on weekends and federal holidays.)

Prospective renters may talk to a Cabins Desk volunteer Monday through Friday from 11:30 am to 1:30 pm at 703-242-0315 ext. 102 or e-mail Cabinsdesk@patc.net

LAND STEWARDSHIP

PATC cabins are located either on private properties or on public land a state or federal agency owns, such as Shenandoah National Park.

With those PATC cabins on public parkland, PATC enters into a memorandum of agreement with the state or federal agency to have exclusive use of a particular cabin(s). These agreements are periodically renewed.

Private land can be either property PATC owns or another landowner owns and leases to PATC. As of the date of this printing, PATC leases two properties and their cabins (Dunlodge and Vining Cabin) from the Daniel and Motoko Vining family.

All of the other cabins on private land are owned by PATC (except Bears Den Cottage). PATC currently is working to place conservation easements on many of these properties to permanently preserve their natural wilderness settings.

Most of the properties PATC owns were acquired by the Club to protect a public trail from being closed by a private landowner, or to prevent residences from being built next to the trail thereby destroying a hiker's feeling of remoteness. Many times PATC has purchased a property to provide public parking for hikers or to ensure legal access to a public park. Examples are the Meadows property in Madison County, Virginia and the Entry Run property in Greene County, Virginia. Sometimes a cabin is already on the trail land being acquired and PATC's cabins construction crew will restore it as a members-only rental cabin. Or a cabin may be disassembled and moved to a PATC trail property, such as the Old Rag Cabin that is located next to the public parking lot the National Park Service established to accommodate hiker vehicles.

The first cabins that PATC managed were in Shenandoah National Park: Range View (built in 1933); Rock Spring (built in 1936); and Doyles River and Pocosin (built in 1937). Also in 1937, Milesburn Cabin in Pennsylvania became available for PATC use. In 1939, PATC owned its first cabin—Bear Spring—as the result of a gift from Harrison Krider. Since then, the club has obtained other cabins through gift or purchase. There are now 42 rentable cabins that are either owned or managed by PATC.

Cabin acquisition has contributed to PATC's status as a major conservation property owner in the Mid-Atlantic States. The club's conservation responsibilities include several leased properties and lands containing trail and scenic easements.

PATC acquires land based on three principles: 1) to protect PATC-maintained trails; 2) to protect the environment surrounding PATC trails; and 3) to enhance recreational purposes. PATC properties are managed under the principles of conservation and environmental stewardship.

VINING TRACT HISTORY

PATC has six cabins on property known as the Vining Tract on the eastern slope of the Blue Ridge Mountains north of Charlottesville, Virginia. These cabins are Mutton Top, Morris, Johnson, Wineberry, Conley, and Vining.

In 1979 a real estate appraiser, and also an active PATC member and trail overseer, A. P. (Sandy) Grice, was working on land acquisition for the Appalachian Trail corridor. While researching property values in the Greene County Courthouse in Stanardsville, Virginia, he discovered a large tract of land for sale. After hiking around it, he was convinced PATC was the ideal candidate to preserve the cabins there and use the property to its best advantage. He contacted PATC Lands Acquisition Chairman Phil Paschall with the information. In 1981 a mutually acceptable deal was forged with Dr. and Mrs. Rutledge Vining, for whom the property is now named. At 249 acres, the Vining Tract is PATC's second-largest land holding (after Great North Mountain).

Dr. Vining was a professor at the University of Virginia and acquired the property early in the 1950s. The Vinings used Morris Cabin as their personal retreat. They granted a life estate to Elijah Conley and allowed the William Craddock family to build a cabin on the upper meadow—Mutton Top Cabin. It was Dr. and Mrs. Vining's express wish that the buyer of their land preserve the many vestiges of the century-old Appalachian settlement scattered across the property including cemeteries, stone and split-rail fences, foundations, terraces, and the cabins. They also wanted to preserve the mountain environment, forests, pastures, orchards, and other physical features of the land. Dr. Vining passed away in 1999 at the age of 91.

The Vining Cabin reflects Dr. and Mrs. Vining's wish to preserve the many vestiges of the century-old Appalachian settlement scattered across their property, including cemeteries, stone and split-rail fences, foundations, terraces, and the cabins.

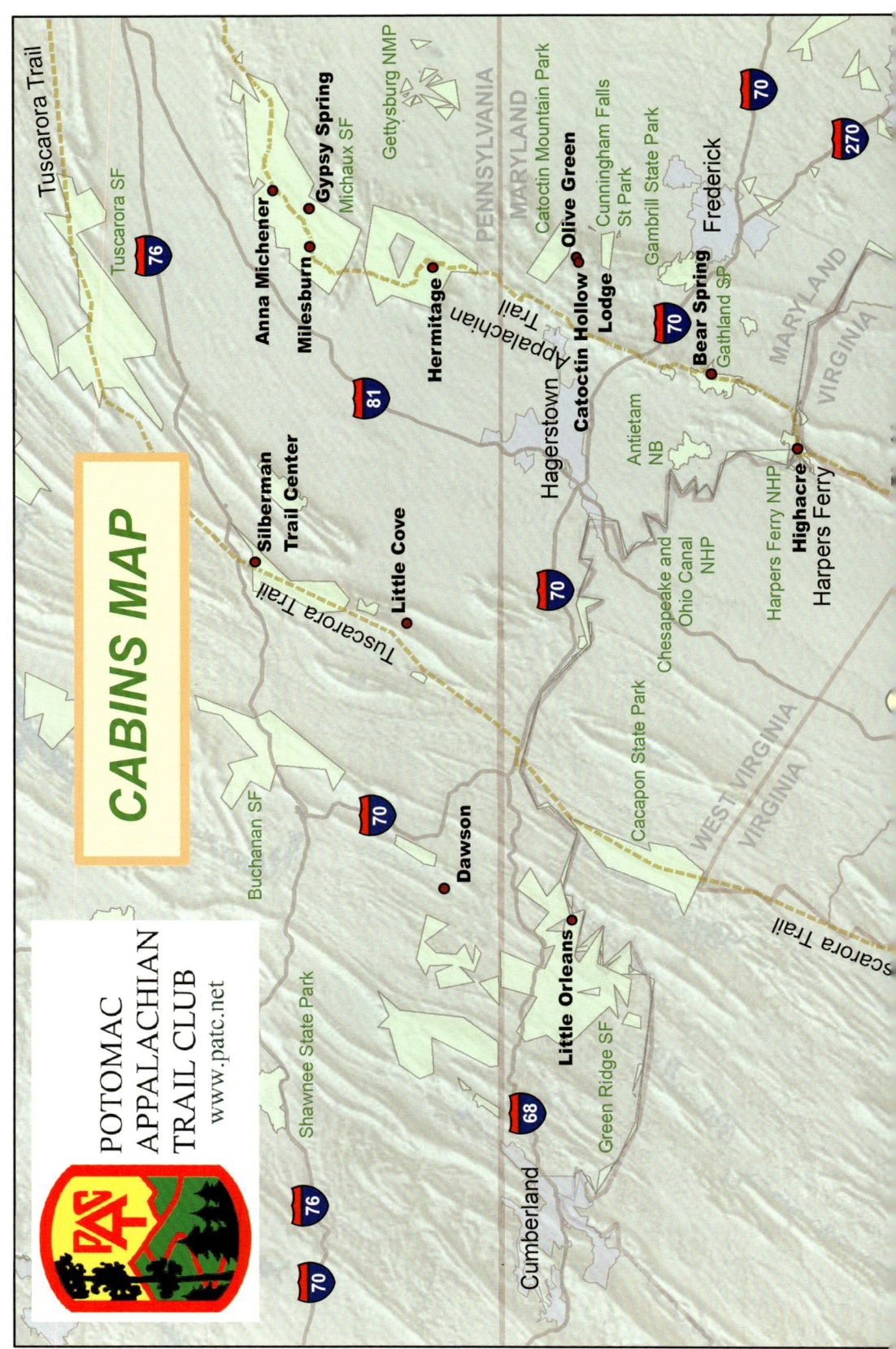

PATC Cabins At-a-Glance

Public Cabin
PATC Member-Only Cabin

 Anna Michener Cabin 24
 Argow Cabin 86
 Bear Spring Cabin 42
 Bears Den Cottage Cabin 48

 Blackburn Trail Center 46
 Catoctin Hollow Lodge 38
 Cliff's House Cabin 74
 Conley Cabin 100

 Corbin Cabin 66
 Dawson Cabin 34
 Doyles River Cabin 90
 Dunlodge 104

 Glass House Cabin 54
 Gypsy Spring Cabin 28
 The Hermitage Cabin 32
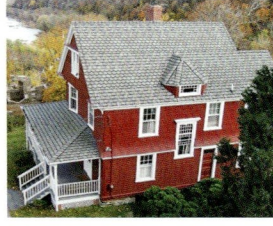 Highacre House 44

 Horwitz Cabin 56
 Huntley House Cabin 64
 John's Rest Cabin 84 
 Johnson Cabin 96

20 POTOMAC APPALACHIAN TRAIL CLUB CABINS

 Jones Mountain Cabin 78	 Lambert Cabin 60	 Little Cove Cabin 30	 Little Orleans Cabin 36
 Meadows Cabin 72	 Milesburn Cabin 26	 Morris Cabin 94	 Mutton Top Cabin 92
 Myron Glaser Cabin 50	 Old Rag Cabin 68	 Olive Green Cabin 40	 Pocosin Cabin 80
 Range View Cabin 58	 Robert Humphrey Cabin 76	 Rock Spring Cabin 70	 Rosser Lamb Cabin 82
 Schairer Trail Center 88	 Silberman Trail Center 22	 Sugar Knob Cabin 52	 Tulip Tree Cabin 62
 Vining Cabin 102	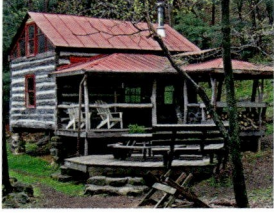 Wineberry Cabin 98		

POTOMAC APPALACHIAN TRAIL CLUB CABINS   **21**

CABIN TYPE: Primitive

CAPACITY: 8

LOCATION: Near Cowans Gap State Park, PA, north of Fort Louden, PA

MAP: PATC Map K

BUNKS & BEDS: Mattresses provided for 8 persons; 1 double bed, 1 double-deck bunk, and space on loft floor

COOKING: Wood stove; summer kitchen next to cabin with grill

HEAT: Wood stove (do not try to heat cabin with fireplace)

OUTSIDE FIRE: In fire pit only or grill in summer kitchen

WATER: Three sources of water; closest source is often dry so renters should bring their own water

TOILET: Outhouse

ELECTRICITY: No

PETS: Yes

PATC Member-Only Cabin

Silberman Trail Center

The trail center is located on PATC's Aughwick Creek Tract, a 54-acre mostly wooded parcel of land purchased by the Club in 2004. The Club land is crossed by Aughwick Creek, a splendid trout stream, and is bordered on the southeast by the Buchanan State Forest. The Tuscarora Trail goes along this border, only 100 yards uphill from the cabin. This log cabin was built from a kit by nearly 50 volunteers who donated approximately 5,000 hours of time and completed in 2007. Dr. William Silberman donated the kit to the PATC and the cabin is named in his honor in thanks for that generous gift.

Getting there: There are several routes to reach the cabin, which is near Cowans Gap State Park. Access can be from I-81, I-70, US-30, US-522, PA-75, or the Pennsylvania Turnpike. The cabin is off a paved secondary road, one-half mile up a narrow dirt road. If renters do not want to drive up this road, they can park at the gate and hike in .5 mile. The final 200 yards up this road are steep with sharp curves, so some renters park at the alternate parking area below the cabin and walk up from there. There is space for four to five cars in the parking area at the cabin, and many more cars can park in the overflow parking area at the lower level.

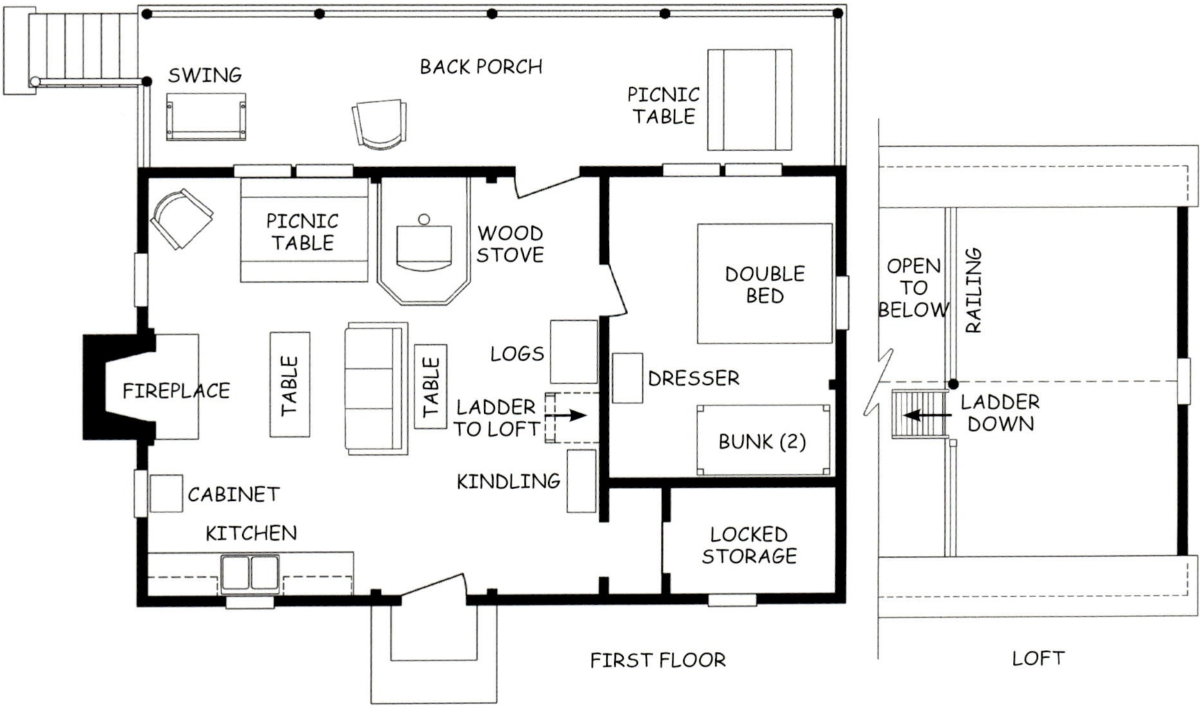

First Floor

- Back Porch (Swing, Picnic Table)
- Picnic Table
- Wood Stove
- Fireplace
- Table, Table
- Logs, Kindling
- Ladder to Loft
- Cabinet
- Kitchen
- Double Bed
- Dresser
- Bunk (2)
- Locked Storage

Loft

- Open to Below
- Railing
- Ladder Down

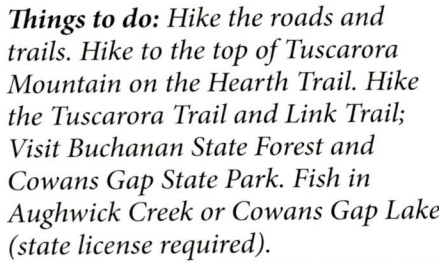

Things to do: *Hike the roads and trails. Hike to the top of Tuscarora Mountain on the Hearth Trail. Hike the Tuscarora Trail and Link Trail; Visit Buchanan State Forest and Cowans Gap State Park. Fish in Aughwick Creek or Cowans Gap Lake (state license required).*

CABINS IN PENNSYLVANIA

CABIN TYPE: Primitive

CAPACITY: 14

LOCATION: On northwest side of South Mountain in Michaux State Forest, 6.6 miles southeast of Shippensburg, PA

MAP: PATC Map 2-3; 0.25 mile to AT by connector trail

BUNKS & BEDS: 2 bunkrooms, each with 3 double-deck bunks and 1 single bunk

COOKING: Wood stove; outdoor grill

HEAT: Fireplace with wood stove insert

OUTSIDE FIRE: In outdoor grill or fire pit only

WATER: Tarkettle Spring is a short distance from the cabin; in dry weather, the spring is further down the trail

TOILET: Outhouse

ELECTRICITY: No

PETS: Yes

Anna Michener Cabin

Anna Michener Cabin is a three-room cabin located on South Mountain about 5 miles from Pine Grove Furnace Cabin to the north and Milesburn Cabin to the south. It is a mile from Tumbling Run Game Preserve, a private inholding within the Michaux State Forest. Michener Cabin was built between 1963 and 1966 by members and friends of PATC and was dedicated to Anna M. Michener, a long-time member, ardent trail worker, and Club office holder.

The cabin today still reflects, despite heavy use, the careful workmanship that went into its construction. The cabin has a cheerful and spacious living room with a fireplace containing a wood-stove insert, and two separate bunkrooms. With ample space, the cabin is good for families, although it can be hard to heat in severe cold weather.

Getting there: The cabin is east of Ridge Road and an unmarked forest road off of the Arendtsville-Shippensburg Road. Parking for about four cars is before the gate and crossing of the Appalachian Trail (AT). The hike-in to the cabin is 1.4 miles via the AT and a short side trail.

Attention: Tumbling Run Game Preserve is private; hikers must respect its privacy.

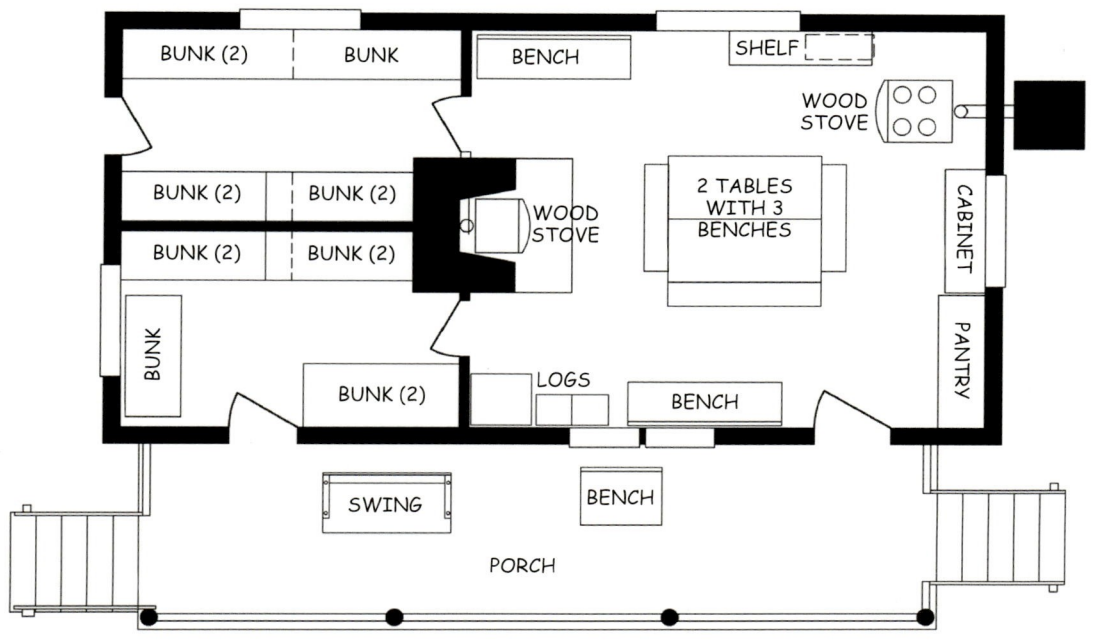

Things to do: The AT is a short distance from the cabin. At 1.4 miles south on the AT is the Big Flat fire tower on Ridge Road. For potential wildlife viewing, go left (north) down the Big Pond Road from beyond the fire tower. Sunset Rocks Trail is also a good hike. See also PATC's "Circuit Hikes in Virginia, West Virginia, Maryland, and Pennsylvania."

CABIN TYPE: Primitive

CAPACITY: 10

LOCATION: On northwest side of South Mountain in Michaux State Forest, 7.0 miles southeast of Shippensburg, PA

MAP: PATC Map 2-3; 60 feet to AT by connector trail

BUNKS & BEDS: On second floor, 1 double bed in first room, 2 double-deck bunks and 4 bunks in 2 other rooms

COOKING: Wood cook stove

HEAT: Wood cook stove and wood stove/fireplace insert

OUTSIDE FIRE: In fire pit only

WATER: Spring is 200 feet downstream of cabin

TOILET: Outhouse

ELECTRICITY: No

PETS: Yes

Milesburn Cabin

Milesburn is located in the center of Michaux State Forest, 6.0 miles southeast of Shippensburg, PA. It is only 60 feet from the AT and Milesburn Road. The cabin was built in 1930 in the just-established Michaux State Forest, near the head of Milesburn Hollow; predating the AT and even Milesburn Road. It was a ranger cabin, then a lodge for a hunting club, and was first used by PATC in 1934, making it one of the oldest cabins in the club. Since 1937, the year the AT was completed, it has been used exclusively in the PATC cabins system under lease from the Pennsylvania Department of Environmental Resources. Michaux State Forest is now more than 85,000 acres. There is a small seasonal stream and footbridge at the front of the cabin, and spring water is not far away. There are lots of area activities from playing in the seasonal stream in front of the cabin to hiking the AT. Wildlife is abundant in the area.

Getting there: The cabin is on Milesburn Road, a long dirt road that can be approached from either the west or east side of Michaux State Forest. From the west, Milesburn Road is off of Baltimore Road, east of Shippensburg. From the east, Milesburn Road is off of PA-233, Pine Grove Road, north of Caledonia State Park. Milesburn Road crosses the AT close to the cabin. There is parking space for four cars at the cabin.

Attention: Milesburn Road is not cleared when it snows.

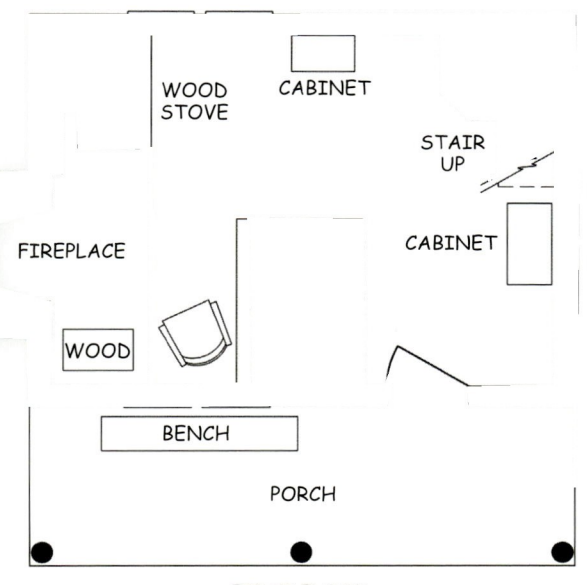

FIRST FLOOR

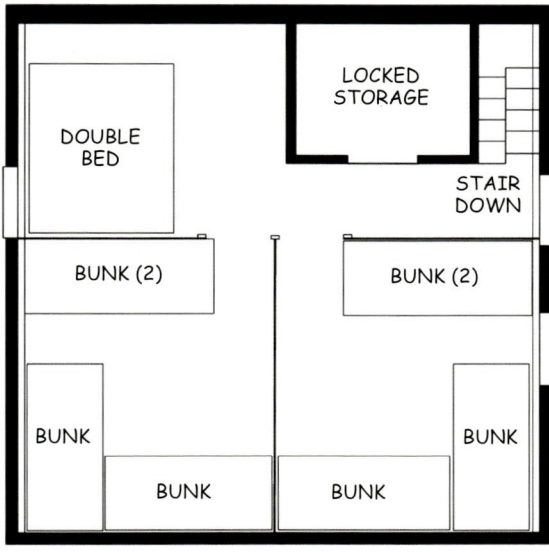

SECOND FLOOR

Things to do: *Hikes in either direction along the AT are interesting and pass through Michaux State Forest's historic and present day experimental plantations. The highest point on the AT in Pennsylvania is just 1 mile southwest on top of Big Pine Flat Ridge at 2,080 feet. There are many forest trails and roads in the area, frequented by hikers, horseback riders, cross country skiers, and mountain bikers. Rocky Knob Trail provides a good loop hike of approximately 6 miles. PATC and other maps are available at the Caledonia State Park office on PA-233.*

CABIN TYPE: Modern

CAPACITY: 6

LOCATION: About 10 miles west of Biglerville, PA

MAP: PATC Map 2-3; 1.2 miles to AT by trail

BUNKS & BEDS: 2 double-deck bunks and 1 double bed

COOKING: Electric stove and oven, microwave, and refrigerator

HEAT: Wood stove and electric baseboard heat

OUTSIDE FIRE: In fire pit only

WATER: Well water from the faucets

TOILET: Bathroom with sink, shower, toilet

ELECTRICITY: Yes

PETS: Yes

PATC Member-Only Cabin

Gypsy Spring Cabin

Gypsy Spring Cabin is a fully equipped facility disguised as a rustic cottage nestled in the center of Pennsylvania's Michaux State Forest. The property was bequeathed to PATC in 1997 by long-time and noted member Ray Fadner, who built the frame and log structure as his personal retreat in the 1970s. Ray also worked with the rangers at Michaux State Forest and Caledonia State Park.

The renovated cottage has three rooms and a full bath. The kitchen is equipped with electric stove, microwave, refrigerator, and hot and cold running water. The living room/dining area is compact with a wood-burning stove (the primary heat source) and supplemented electric baseboard heat. A patio door opens onto the covered porch with a view (when the leaves have fallen) of distant Gettysburg. The cabin is good for families, although the wood stove gets very hot and can be a danger to small children.

Getting there: The drive is on paved roads and winding, country roads. The driveway is unpaved and there is parking for up to eight cars at the cabin.

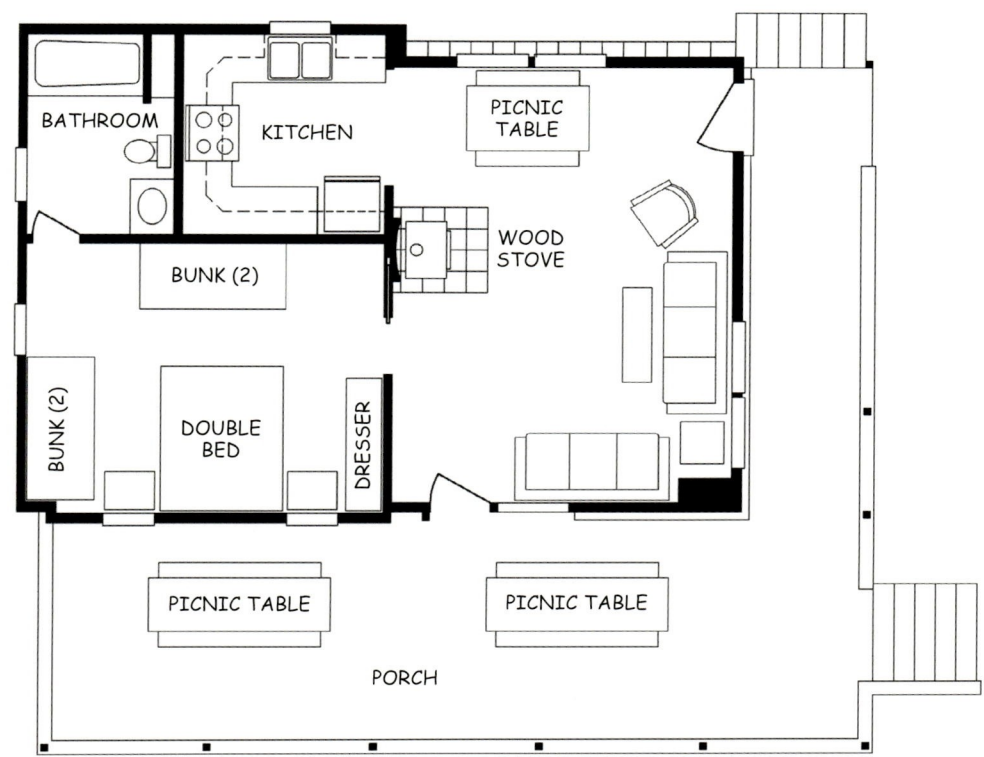

Things to do: *Hikes in either direction along the AT are interesting, passing Michaux State Forest experimental plantations. Hike or do other recreational opportunities in the Michaux State Forest or Caledonia State Park. Evening programs at nearby Caledonia or Pine Grove Furnace State Parks offer interesting and informational opportunities for visitors during the summer.*

CABINS IN PENNSYLVANIA

CABIN TYPE: Modern

CAPACITY: 8

LOCATION: About 6 miles west of Mercersburg, PA

MAP: PATC Map K; 1.5 miles to Tuscarora Trail by trail

BUNKS & BEDS: 2 single beds, 2 double beds, 1 double-deck bunk

COOKING: Electric range with oven, microwave, and refrigerator; outdoor fire pit with grill

HEAT: Electric baseboard heater in bathroom and fireplace

OUTSIDE FIRE: In fire pit only

WATER: Well water pumped to cabin sinks and shower

TOILET: Bathroom with sink, toilet, and shower

ELECTRICITY: Yes

PETS: Yes

PATC Member-Only Cabin

Little Cove Cabin

Little Cove Cabin is located on a 160-acre tract of wooded mountain ground in Warren Township, Franklin County, Pennsylvania. By foot trail, it is 1.5 miles from the Tuscarora Trail, which runs along the top of Tuscarora Mountain on Pennsylvania State Game Lands #124. The cabin is situated in a picturesque mountain valley with a stream flowing nearby and Tuscarora Mountain located at the back side of the property.

The property, purchased by PATC in February 2010, came with an existing cabin, which although structurally sound was in need of extensive repairs. In 2013, much of the interior and exterior was remodeled, with a large covered porch added on three sides of the cabin being the most notable feature. Some of the neighboring properties include a church camp and Pennsylvania state game lands.

Getting there: The cabin is west of Mercersburg, off of PA-16 and PA-456. The slate access road for the cabin rises steeply from the valley floor and is cut by several water bars (drainage ditches). It is recommended that those with lower clearance vehicles proceed carefully up the road. There is space for about four cars in the parking area by the cabin.

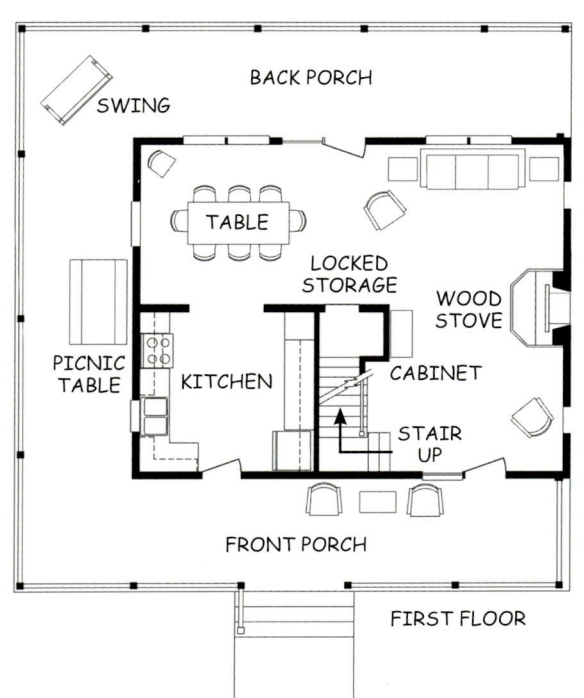

FIRST FLOOR

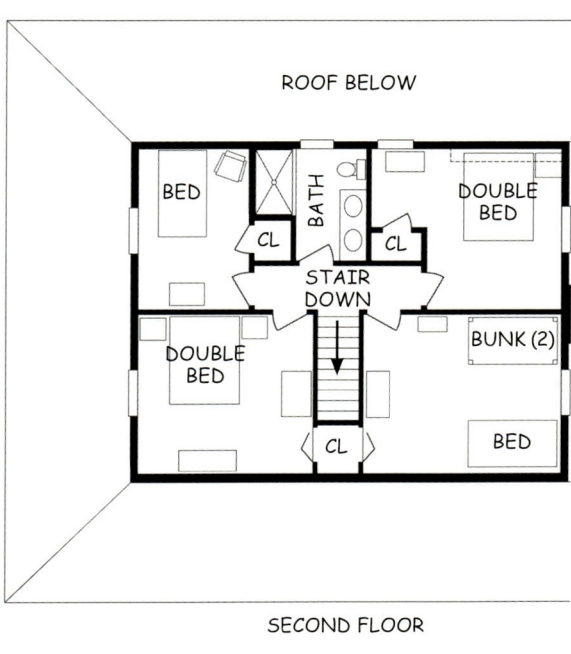

SECOND FLOOR

Things to do: Hike the roads and trails on the property. Hike to the Reese Hollow Shelter at the back of the property. Hike to the top of Tuscarora Mountain where the local trails join the Tuscarora Trail running along the crest of the mountain.

CABINS IN PENNSYLVANIA   31

CABIN TYPE: Primitive

CAPACITY: 8

LOCATION: Michaux State Forest, South Mountain area, about 6 miles north of Waynesboro, PA

MAP: PATC Map 4; 0.7 mile to AT by trail

BUNKS & BEDS: 1 double-width, double-deck bunk on main floor; room for 6 mattresses on loft floor

COOKING: Wood stove and fireplace insert; outside fire grill

HEAT: Wood stove and fireplace insert

OUTSIDE FIRE: In grill only

WATER: Short path from cabin to PVC pipe at the stream; all-year spring is near the parking area; small spring, usually unreliable in dry periods, is located across Tumbling Run

TOILET: Outhouse

ELECTRICITY: No

PETS: Yes

The Hermitage Cabin

This one-room frame cabin in Pennsylvania's Michaux State Forest was rebuilt by PATC volunteers from 1975–77. The cabin overlooks Tumbling Run, which flows beneath hemlocks near the bottom of a forested ravine near Snowy Mountain. Rocky cliffs, often used by technical rock climbers, overlook the cabin. An outside shower stall is available for those willing to heat additional water carried uphill from the stream. A partial loft supplements the main-floor bunks. The steep, ladder-like, loft stairway might be dangerous for small children or sleepwalkers.

   Getting there: The Monument Park-Shaffer Rock parking area for the cabin is on Swift Run Road, which is west of Old Forge Road. The hike-in is 0.25 mile but is very steep and rocky. The cabin can also be reached via side trails from the AT.

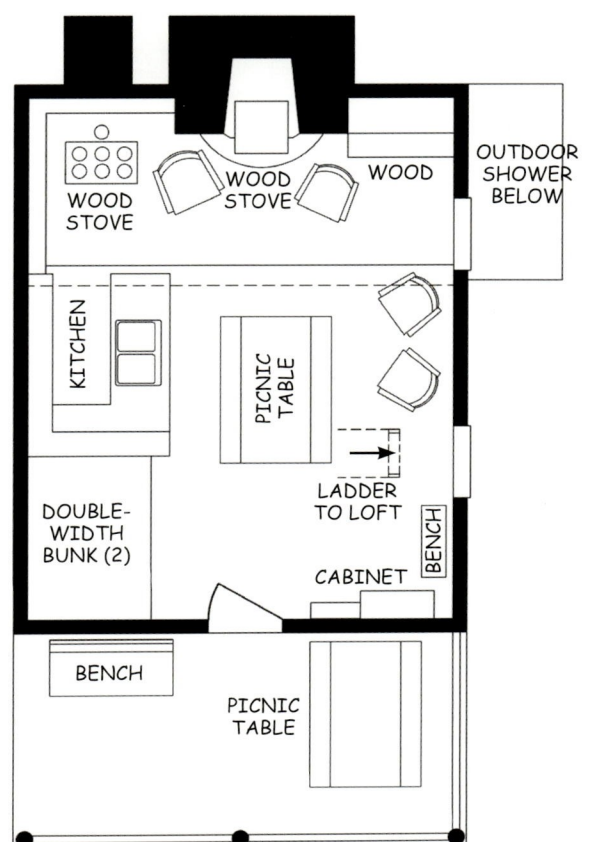

MAIN FLOOR

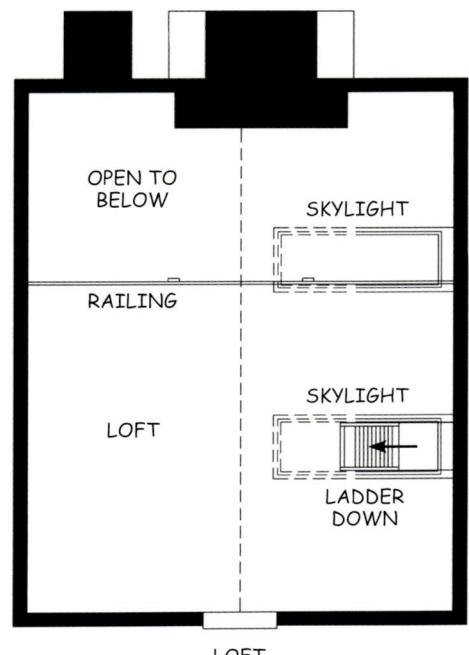

LOFT

Things to do: *Hike along Tumbling Run, the AT, and in the State Forest. Caledonia State Park and Gettysburg are nearby.*

CABINS IN PENNSYLVANIA **33**

CABIN TYPE: Primitive

CAPACITY: 7

LOCATION: About 5 miles east of Chaneysville, PA, on the east side of Buchanan State Forest

MAP: Buchanan State Forest public use map; USGS Chaneysville, PA, Quadrangle, 7.5 Minute Series; cabin is not close to the AT

BUNKS & BEDS: 1 double-width, double-deck bunk, 1 double-deck bunk, 1 long bunk

COOKING: Wood stove and outdoor fire pit

HEAT: Wood stove

OUTSIDE FIRE: In fire pit only

WATER: There is not a reliable water source at the cabin so please bring any necessary water

TOILET: Outhouse

ELECTRICITY: No

PETS: Yes

Dawson Cabin

This light and airy two-room frame cabin was donated to PATC by the Dawson family in memory of Charles Dawson, a member of the Club's Cabin Construction Committee and an AT through-hiker. Charlie built the cabin shell and furnished it austerely for his own use during the 1970s. Club work crews insulated and paneled the interior and built and installed furnishings for group occupancy. A twelve-foot picture window across most of one side of the main room makes this one of the brightest of all the PATC cabins. The cabin stands on a cleared knoll with a beautiful view to the south, toward Green Ridge, and to the southeast, toward Sideling Hill.

The cabin adjoins Buchanan State Forest (primarily a pine plantation) affording opportunities to explore abandoned farm sites and to climb to the ridge line of Big Mountain with views westward to the Alleghenies. Young children should enjoy playing on the open knoll. The site is not too far from the Tuscarora Trail or from skiing.

Getting there: The cabin is off of PA-26, which is north of exit 68/Orleans Road on I-68. There is a small gravel parking area for four cars right off of PA-26 near Piney Creek. The hike-in is up the hill for approximately 0.2 mile.

Attention: There is not a reliable water source at the cabin, so bring any necessary water. There is an intermittent spring about 1,000 feet north and downhill from the cabin. Water from the nearby stream passes through pasture land and should be boiled or treated before use. Rob Spring, 1.1 miles due west of the cabin, may be reached by a trail that follows the ridge west from the cabin and joins a woods road (to left) that passes the spring.

The ceiling is insulated with Styrofoam. Do not hang any heat-producing lanterns near the ceiling.

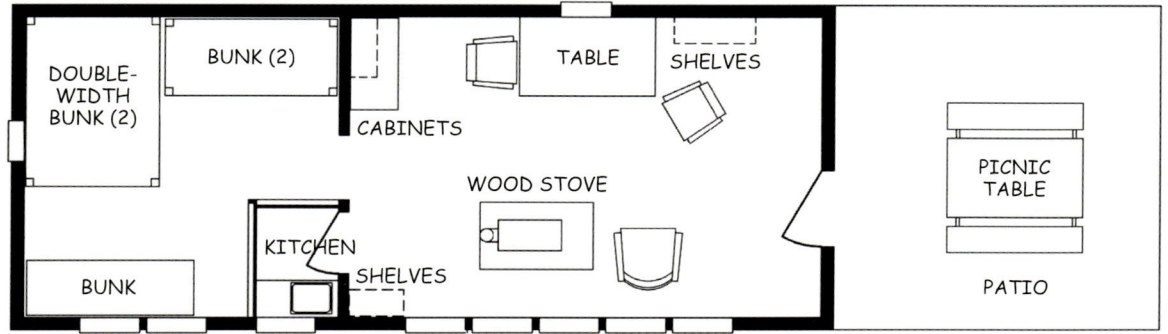

> ***What to do:*** *Hike state forest roads and trails; explore abandoned farm sites and climb to the ridge line of Big Mountain, which gives views westward toward the Allegheny Mountains.*

CABIN TYPE: Semi-primitive

CAPACITY: 8

LOCATION: 20 miles west of Hancock, MD

MAP: No PATC Map; no trail to AT

BUNKS & BEDS: 8 mattresses for use in upstairs loft and living room

COOKING: Electric cook stove; electric refrigerator

HEAT: Wood-burning stove

OUTSIDE FIRE: Fire pit and grill

WATER: Potable pumped well water with hot and cold running water in kitchen; shower available from April to November

TOILET: Outhouse

ELECTRICITY: Yes, lights, refrigerator, and stove

PETS: Yes

PATC Member-Only Cabin

Little Orleans Cabin

The Little Orleans Cabin is located near Little Orleans, Maryland, about 20 miles west of Hancock. It is situated on a 37-acre tract that adjoins National Park Service property (the C&O Canal National Historical Park and the abandoned right-of-way of the Western Maryland Railroad). The cabin sits in a meadow and is close to the Potomac River and C&O Canal Towpath, but is separated from those by a ridge. The cabin setting is private and peaceful.

The cabin is a frame structure, with a kitchen, living room, upstairs sleeping loft, and a narrow, east-facing porch shaded by evergreens and a walnut tree. A ceiling fan in the living room aids air circulation. For those who are considering a family get-away, it is the opinion of many that Little Orleans is the most child-friendly cabin in the PATC system. It is easy to get to and has a large open area around it where kids can be easily supervised while playing.

Getting there: From I-68, the cabin is south of Little Orleans, Maryland and the Fifteen Mile Creek Campground. The cabin access road is dirt and there is parking for four to five cars at the cabin. The driveway is fairly narrow with a sharp drop off on the left. Please take caution, especially in wet or snowy weather. The cabin can also be reached via hike-in from the C&O Canal Towpath.

Attention: The cabin key unlocks a storage shed near the cabin. It contains a hammock, a croquet set, a lawn mower, and a fuel can. Renters are encouraged to help keep the grass cut. It makes for a nicer stay.

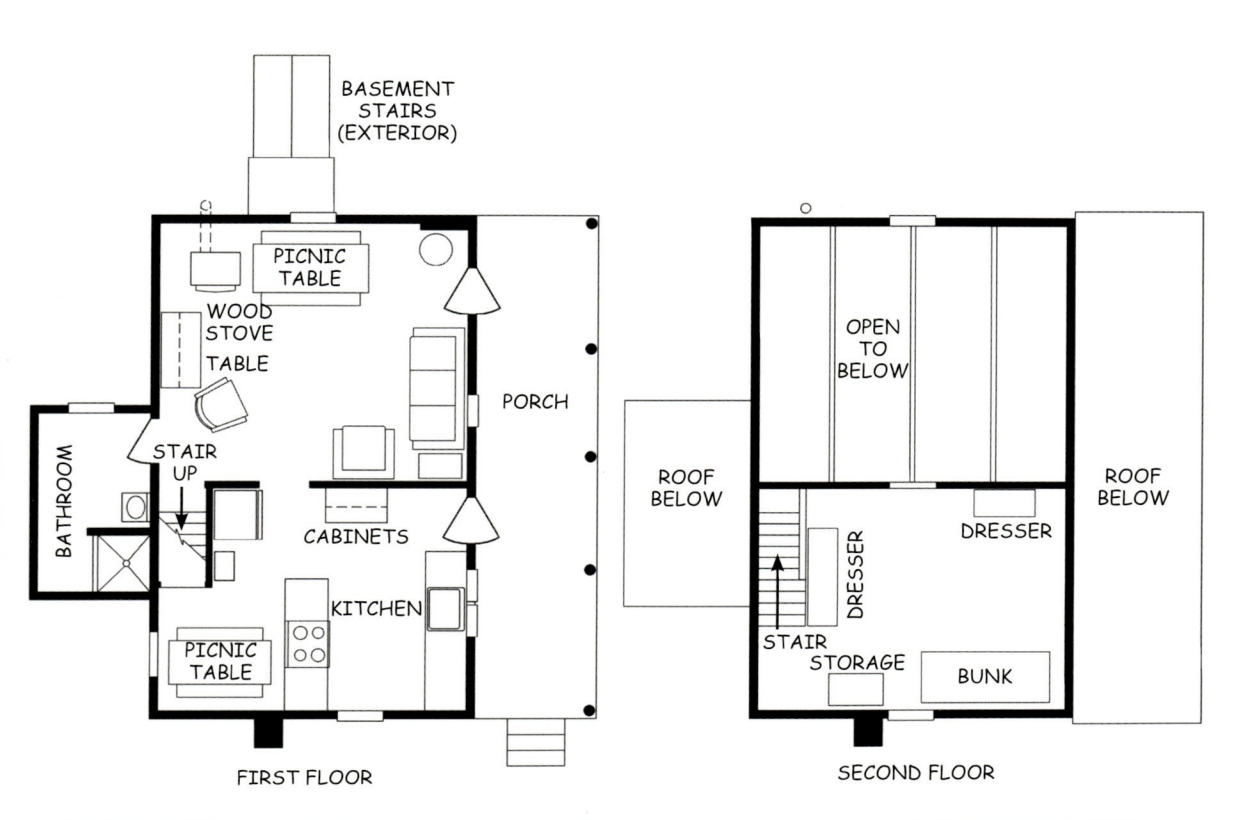

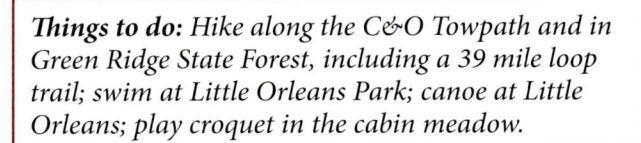

FIRST FLOOR

- BASEMENT STAIRS (EXTERIOR)
- PICNIC TABLE
- WOOD STOVE
- TABLE
- BATHROOM
- STAIR UP
- PORCH
- CABINETS
- KITCHEN
- PICNIC TABLE

SECOND FLOOR

- OPEN TO BELOW
- ROOF BELOW
- ROOF BELOW
- DRESSER
- DRESSER
- STAIR
- STORAGE
- BUNK

Things to do: Hike along the C&O Towpath and in Green Ridge State Forest, including a 39 mile loop trail; swim at Little Orleans Park; canoe at Little Orleans; play croquet in the cabin meadow.

CABINS IN MARYLAND 37

CABIN TYPE: Modern

CAPACITY: 8

LOCATION: Cunningham Falls State Park, about 3 miles west of Thurmont, MD

MAP: PATC Maps 5-6; no trail to AT

BUNKS & BEDS: Double bed and 2 twin beds downstairs; double bed and 2 twin beds upstairs

COOKING: Electric stove/oven, refrigerator, dishwasher, and microwave

HEAT: Central heating and air conditioning; fireplace

OUTSIDE FIRE: In fire ring only

WATER: Hot and cold running water from well

TOILET: 2 full bathrooms

ELECTRICITY: Yes

PETS: No

Catoctin Hollow Lodge

The lodge is a modern three bedroom log house built in 1988. The Lok-n-Logs Inc. kit construction includes a great room with 22-foot ceilings and a stone fireplace. The first floor has a full kitchen, sunroom, two bedrooms, and a full bath. The second floor contains a loft, bedroom, and a second full bath. There is a covered front porch with a wrap-around deck, a nice yard with room for play, and a fire ring. The Lodge also has air conditioning.

Thanks to the generosity of PATC members in the 2014 year-end fund drive and countless PATC volunteer hours, the Lodge has been restored to tip-top shape so that renters will enjoy and cherish this gem in the woods of Cunningham Falls State Park in northern Maryland. It is a perfect spot for those who love the great outdoors without leaving behind the comforts of home. The Lodge property is adjacent to the Olive Green Cabin and the Catoctin Trail.

The Lodge is currently owned by the State of Maryland Department of Natural Resources which has leased it to the PATC to make it available to the general public and PATC members. The property adjoins Cunningham Falls State Park and renters can access the park's amenities (additional fee(s) may apply).

Getting there: Cunningham Falls State Park is approximately 3 miles west of Thurmont, Maryland. The cabin is near the William Houck Area campground, off of Catoctin Hollow Road. There is parking for two cars behind the Campground Entrance Station. The relatively easy hike-in is .75 mile up a gradual incline to the Lodge.

FIRST FLOOR

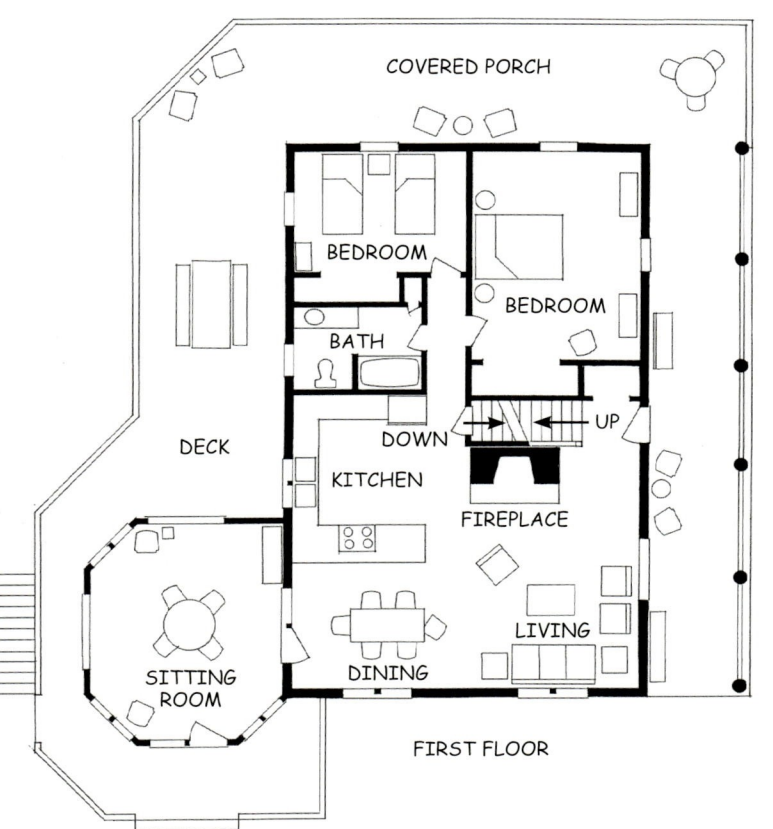

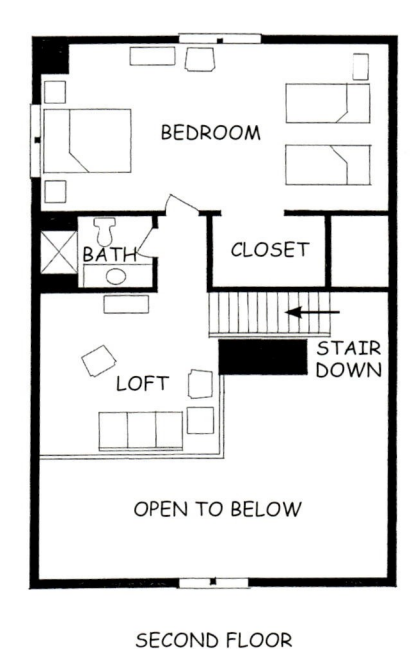

SECOND FLOOR

Things to do: The Catoctin Trail passes near the Lodge and there are many trails in both Cunningham Falls State Park and Catoctin Mountain Park. The park visitors folder, available at the Catoctin Mountain Park Visitors Center, is an excellent guide to park trails and activities. PATC Map 5-6 gives the routes of the Catoctin Trail and the AT (about a 6 mile drive away).

CABINS IN MARYLAND   39

CABIN TYPE: Primitive

CAPACITY: 4

LOCATION: Cunningham Falls State Park, about 3 miles west of Thurmont, MD

MAP: PATC Maps 5-6; no trail to AT

BUNKS & BEDS: 2 double-deck bunks with 4 mattresses and blankets in upstairs sleeping area

COOKING: Wood stove; stone hearth outside

HEAT: Wood stove

OUTSIDE FIRE: In stone hearth only

WATER: In winter, bring drinking water; water for washing can be dipped from the nearby stream. In summer, water is available from a spout at the nearby campground. Water is also available at the Catoctin Mountain Park Visitor Center.

TOILET: Outhouse

ELECTRICITY: No

PETS: No

Olive Green Cabin

This historic cabin was constructed of logs in 1871 and was used by members of the Green family until the cabin and property were acquired in 1986 by the State of Maryland for Cunningham Falls State Park. The cabin is named for its last owner, Mrs. Olive Green, who was a true mountain woman, working with her woodcutter husband on the other end of a two-handled saw. Mrs. Green lived in the cabin until 1986, when she was 83 years old, and raised eight children there. In 1993, the state commissioned PATC volunteers to demolish two additions built onto the original structure when the Green family was growing.

There is a living area downstairs and a sleeping area upstairs. Nearby access to canoe and small boat rentals and Hunting Creek Lake at the William Houck Camping Area in the park make this cabin a favorite with families.

Getting there: Cunningham Falls State Park is about 3 miles west of Thurmont, Maryland. The cabin is next to the William Houck Area campground and picnic area, off of Catoctin Hollow Road. There is room for two cars in the driveway between the road and the chained gate. There is a short walk-in from the gate.

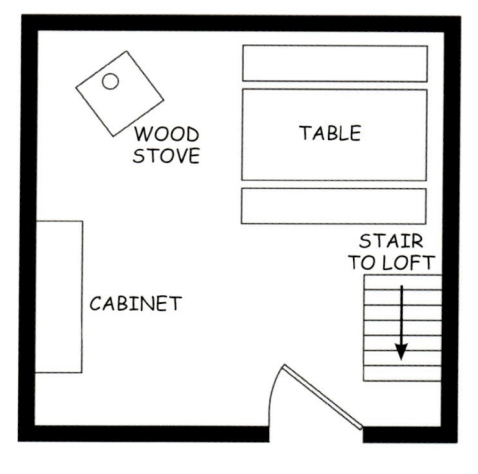

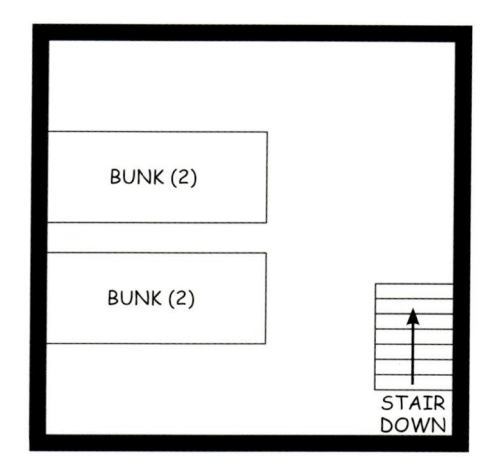

FIRST FLOOR

LOFT

Things to do: The Catoctin Trail passes near the cabin and there are many trails in both Cunningham Falls State Park and Catoctin Mountain Park. The park visitors folder, available at the Catoctin Mountain Park Visitors Center, is an excellent guide to park trails. PATC Map 5-6 gives the routes of the Catoctin Trail and the AT (about a 6 mile drive away).

CABINS IN MARYLAND   41

CABIN TYPE: Primitive

CAPACITY: 6

LOCATION: About 4 miles south of Turners Gap, where Alternate US-40 crosses the AT west of Middletown, MD

MAP: PATC Map 5-6; 0.7 mile to AT by connector trail

BUNKS & BEDS: 2 triple-deck bunks

COOKING: Wood stove; outside grill under cook shed

HEAT: Wood stove

OUTSIDE FIRE: In cook shed grill and designated fire ring only

WATER: Dip from stream nearby or from Bear Spring 0.2 mile up the blue-blazed Bear Spring Trail behind cabin

TOILET: Outhouse

ELECTRICITY: No

PETS: Yes

Bear Spring Cabin

Bear Spring is a simple, one-room log cabin on the eastern slope of South Mountain in Maryland, at the head of Locust Valley. It was one of the first cabins PATC owned, and was offered as a gift, along with 1.5 acres of land, by Mr. Harrison Krider in 1939. The exact age of the cabin is not known, but it was probably built in the early 1930s. PATC members installed a new floor, door, windows, and chinking, as well as bunks and other furnishings.

A short drive from Washington, DC, Bear Spring Cabin is ideal for a small family, although caution should be used with young children sleeping in upper bunks. An indoor wood stove is provided for heating and cooking. A cook shed provides an additional shelter for cooking and dining.

Getting there: The drive to the cabin parking area on Mountain Church Road is several miles past Middletown, Maryland. Park in the church parking lot in one of three spaces designated for Bear Spring Cabin users. The hike-in to the cabin is 0.4 mile. The cabin can also be reached via the AT and Bear Spring Trail. Hike-in is 5.1 miles southward from Turners Gap or 3.7 miles northward from Crampton Gap.

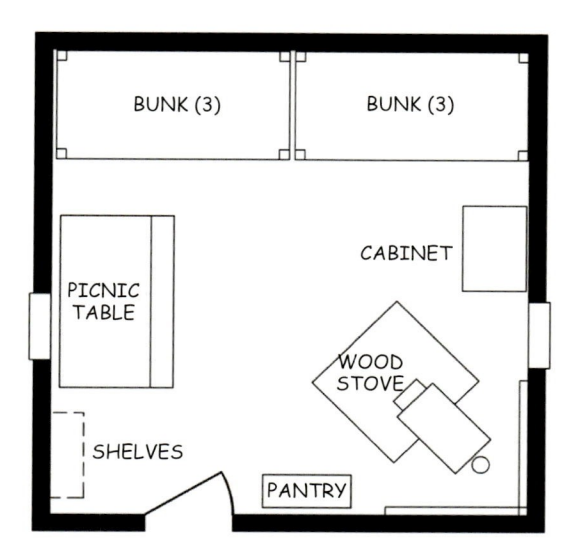

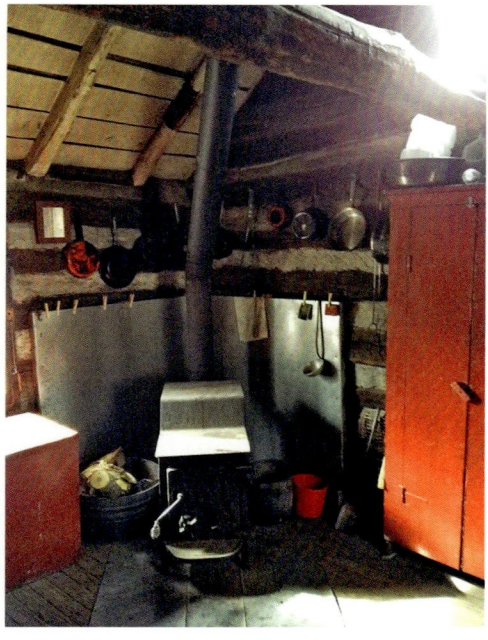

Things to do: Hike along the AT in either direction; hike the White Rocks Trail; hike the short Bear Spring Circuit Trail; visit Washington Monument and Gathland State Parks. See also PATC's "Appalachian Trail Guide to Maryland and Northern Virginia with Side Trails" and "Hikes in Western Maryland."

CABINS IN MARYLAND 43

CABIN TYPE: Modern

CAPACITY: 8

LOCATION: Adjacent to Harpers Ferry National Historic Park, WV and the famous Jefferson Rock

MAP: PATC map 5-6, or 7; 30 feet to AT by connector trail

BUNKS & BEDS: 1 queen bed in front bedroom, 2 single beds in 2 other bedrooms, 1 double bed in back bedroom

COOKING: Electric stove and oven, refrigerator, microwave, and dishwasher; backyard grill

HEAT: Oil furnace

OUTSIDE FIRE: Not allowed

WATER: Hot and cold running water

TOILET: Upstairs bathroom with sink, toilet, and shower

ELECTRICITY: Yes

PETS: No

PATC Member-Only Cabin

Highacre House

Highacre is a comfortable, fully furnished eight-room house in Harpers Ferry, West Virginia that was built in 1887 in the Victorian Cottage style of the era. Originally built for William Luke, Superintendent of the Harpers Ferry Pulp Mill, the house has changed owners only two other times. Kathryn Fulkerson and Marian Lapp, who were respectively PATC's General Secretary and Treasurer in the 1930s, bought the house together and used it as a summer home and PATC gathering place. Kathryn Fulkerson donated Highacre to PATC in 1962. Highacre has been visited by President Grover Cleveland, and in 1998, by President Bill Clinton and Vice President Al Gore, who used the property to access Jefferson Rock to commemorate volunteerism.

Getting there: The driveway to the house veers to the right off of Church Street, where the street levels off after going uphill. Please take extra care in snowy or icy weather as the driveway is steep and curvy. In that situation, it may be best to park at the bottom of the hill and walk up. There is space for about six cars in the parking area next to the house.

Attention: The general rules for cabin users apply to Highacre but there are some additional special rules because of the house's uniqueness. This house and most of the fixtures are over 100 years old and should be treated gently. The furnishings are old as well and should not be used inappropriately. The total number of people using the house during the day is not to exceed 25. *Total* number of people staying overnight, including children of any age is limited to 8. This house is ideal for families with children.

Occupants are responsible for exercising care in their use of the house as well as for leaving it secure, clean, and in good order. The occupant must carry away all garbage and trash. *No burning allowed on the premises and no tent camping is allowed on the grounds.*

FIRST FLOOR

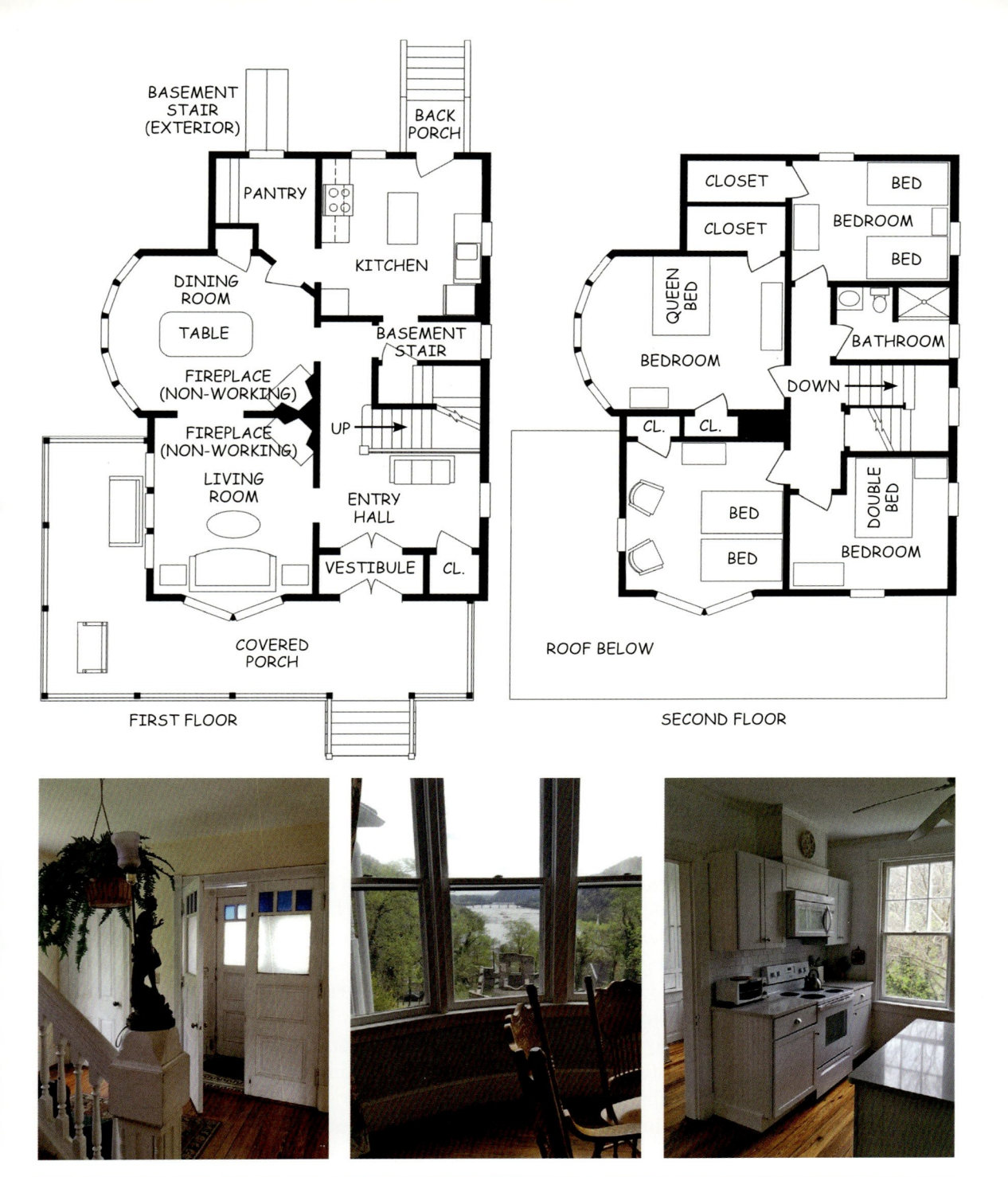

- BASEMENT STAIR (EXTERIOR)
- BACK PORCH
- PANTRY
- KITCHEN
- DINING ROOM
  - TABLE
- BASEMENT STAIR
- FIREPLACE (NON-WORKING)
- FIREPLACE (NON-WORKING)
- UP
- LIVING ROOM
- ENTRY HALL
- VESTIBULE
- CL.
- COVERED PORCH

SECOND FLOOR

- CLOSET
- CLOSET
- BED
- BEDROOM
- BED
- QUEEN BED
- BEDROOM
- BATHROOM
- DOWN
- CL.
- CL.
- BED
- BED
- DOUBLE BED
- BEDROOM
- ROOF BELOW

Things to do: Hikes to Maryland Heights and Loudoun Heights offer spectacular views of the confluence of the Shenandoah and Potomac Rivers; visits to historical places in Harpers Ferry, WV, Shepherdstown, WV, and Antietam, MD provide a sense of the significance of Harpers Ferry in American history. Hiking or biking on the C&O towpath offer other views of this lovely area. For yet another view, spend time relaxing on the front porch or visit the headquarters of the Appalachian Trail Conservancy. For suggestions on other nearby trails see PATC's "Appalachian Trail Guide to Maryland and Northern Virginia with Side Trails."

CABINS IN WEST VIRGINIA/NORTHERN VIRGINIA   45

CABIN TYPE: Semi-primitive

CAPACITY: 22

LOCATION: Just outside Roundhill, VA

MAP: PATC Map 7; 0.25 mile to AT by connector trail

BUNKS & BEDS: 2 bunkrooms upstairs, each with 2 double beds and 2 double-deck bunks and loft with 2 double beds and 3 bunks, all with mattresses; 10 additional single mattresses also available

COOKING: Fully equipped kitchen including: 2 propane kitchen stoves, 2 double sinks, 2 dishwashers, freezer, refrigerator, microwave, toaster, coffeemaker, and 3 dining tables

HEAT: 2 wood stoves for winter heating

OUTSIDE FIRE: Fire ring below lower lawn

WATER: Well water available from tap

TOILET: 2 outhouses; outside solar shower in season

ELECTRICITY: Yes

PETS: No

PATC Member-Only Cabin

Blackburn Trail Center

The Blackburn Trail Center is a wonderful place for a large group to spend a weekend or several days together out in the mountains. It is located on 145 acres and features a main house with a wraparound porch, a large dayroom, huge kitchen, two bunkrooms, and a loft. There is a tent pad on the lower lawn and five tent sites in the woods below the hiker cabin. There are picnic tables on the porch and lawn and a large fire ring below the lower lawn. A mountain road leads right up to the front door of the Center and there is a trailhead parking lot just below the Center.

Resident caretakers live in the carriage house year-round. The Center is primarily designed to support long distance hikers, trail crews, Club planning meetings, and training seminars. When not being used for official Club activities the Center is the perfect location for large group use. Blackburn has hosted weddings, family reunions, and milestone birthday parties. Blackburn is available for rental November through March (closed during the hiking season and for special trail and maintenance crews in the fall).

Getting there: The Blackburn Trail Center is on Appalachian Trail Road outside of Round Hill, Virginia. There is parking for two cars at the Main House and four in the side lot next to the Carriage House. Blackburn is 2.5 miles from the main road and the last mile of the gravel road is straight up the mountain. During winter months snow and ice can make it difficult to drive up. A four-wheel drive vehicle and tire chains are required at such times. If unable to drive up, cars may be parked in the field at the bottom of the mountain. If it is cold and snowy, call the caretaker at the Trail Center for guidance, 540-338-9028. The renter may also call the Cabins Desk for further information.

FIRST FLOOR

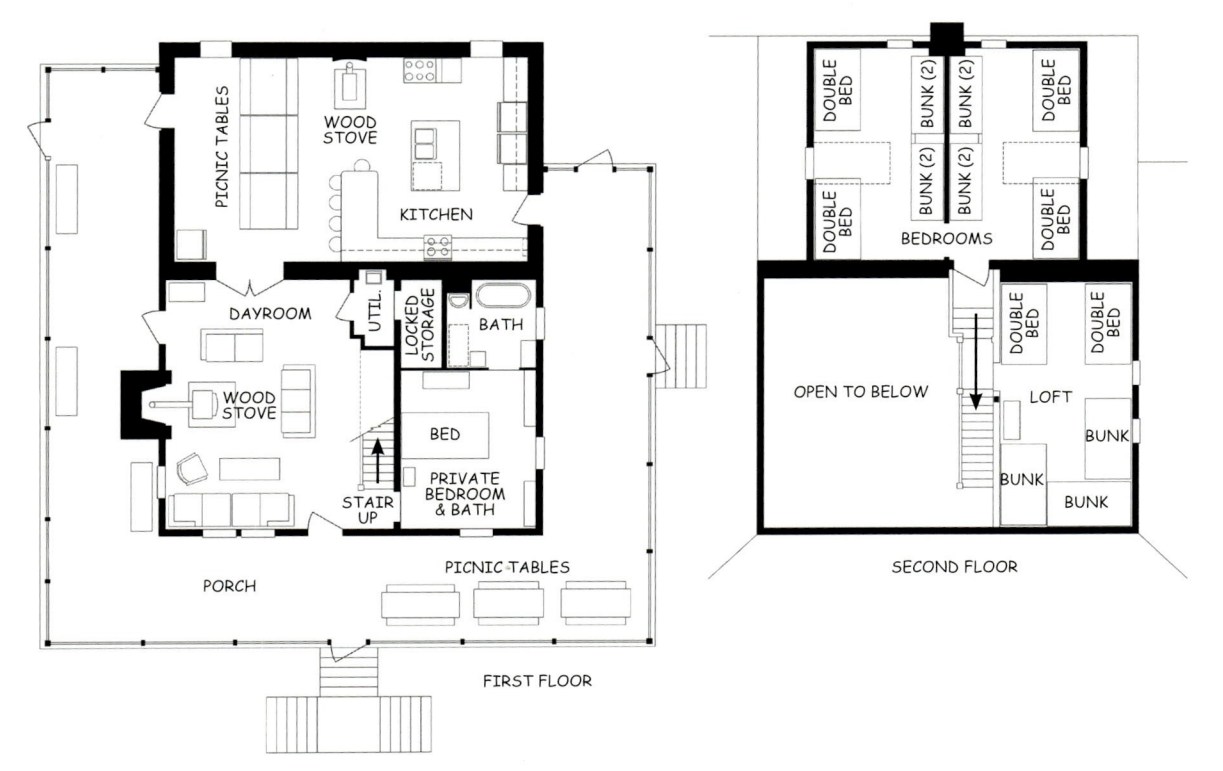

- PICNIC TABLES
- WOOD STOVE
- KITCHEN
- DAYROOM
- UTIL.
- LOCKED STORAGE
- BATH
- WOOD STOVE
- BED
- PRIVATE BEDROOM & BATH
- STAIR UP
- PORCH
- PICNIC TABLES

SECOND FLOOR

- DOUBLE BED
- BUNK (2)
- BUNK (2)
- DOUBLE BED
- DOUBLE BED
- BUNK (2)
- BUNK (2)
- DOUBLE BED
- BEDROOMS
- OPEN TO BELOW
- DOUBLE BED
- DOUBLE BED
- LOFT
- BUNK
- BUNK
- BUNK

Things to do: *Hike on the AT (consult PATC's "Appalachian Trail Guide to Maryland and Northern Virginia with Side Trails"); visit the Appalachian Trail Conservancy in Harpers Ferry, WV; do landscaping work and home improvement projects on Center property.*

CABINS IN WEST VIRGINIA/NORTHERN VIRGINIA   47

CABIN TYPE: Semi-primitive

CAPACITY: 8

LOCATION: 20 miles west of Leesburg, VA south of where the AT crosses VA-7 at Snickers Gap

MAP: PATC Maps 7 and 8; 0.5 mile to AT by connector trail

BUNKS & BEDS: 2 double-deck bunks in bedroom, 2 single mattresses in loft, 2 bunks in main room

COOKING: 2-burner electric cooktop, microwave, refrigerator

HEAT: Fireplace insert

OUTSIDE FIRE: Not allowed

WATER: In warm weather, drinking water is from outside spigot; in cold weather, water is from outside spigot at Bears Den Lodge

TOILET: Outhouse

ELECTRICITY: Yes

PETS: Yes

Bears Den Cottage Cabin

Bears Den Cottage is located on the property of the Bears Den Lodge and Hostel in Loudoun County, Virginia, about 17 miles west of Leesburg. Enjoy the living room fireplace or sitting on the large wooden deck in the middle of the forest. The cottage offers simplicity with a few modern conveniences. It has electricity but no running water. There is an outdoor privy and outdoor water spigot. The cottage, fully furnished, is 600 square feet with one bedroom, overhead loft, and a large main room for kitchen, dining, seating, and reading. Bears Den Cottage is adjacent to the AT.

In April 1984, PATC bought 66 acres of the property that included the cottage and a lodge, later selling the property to the Appalachian Trail Conservancy (ATC). While the ATC still owns the property and the Lodge and Hostel, rental of Bears Den Cottage is managed by PATC.

Getting there: The cottage is on the Bears Den Lodge property, which is off of VA-601, just south of VA-7 at Snickers Gap. Cottage parking is limited to three cars in the Bears Den Lodge day use parking lot. Hike-in from the parking lot is about 0.25 mile downhill.

Note: Bears Den Lodge and Hostel is not part of the PATC cabin system. The lodge and hostel is operated by its own staff and is not connected to the Bears Den Cottage.

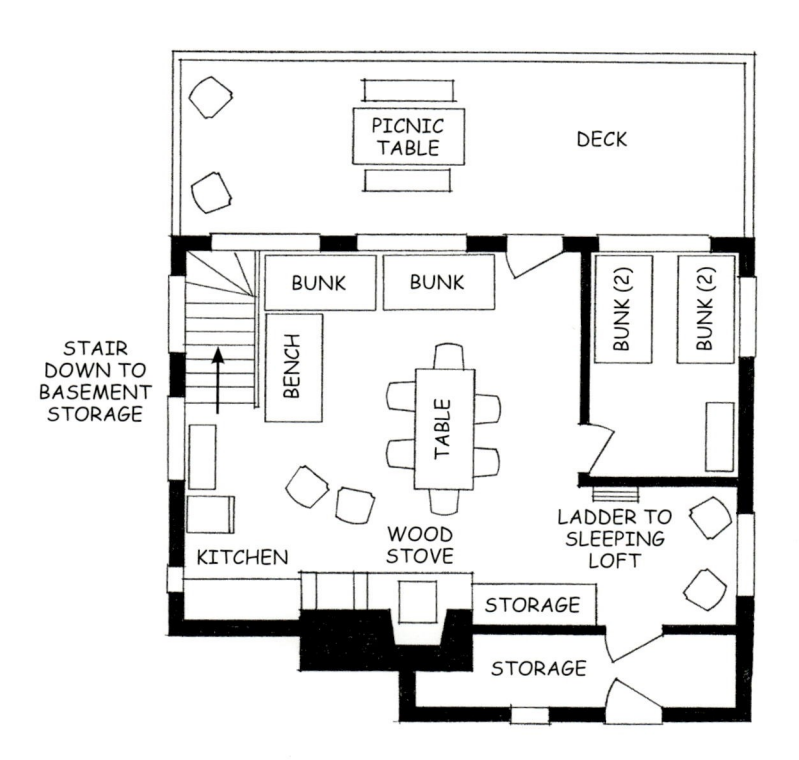

Things to do: Hike on the AT; Bears Den Rocks Overlook offers stunning view of the Shenandoah Valley; stop in at the ATC's Bears Den Lodge and Hostel.

CABINS IN WEST VIRGINIA/NORTHERN VIRGINIA

CABIN TYPE: Primitive

CAPACITY: 12

LOCATION: Western slope of the Blue Ridge, about 2 miles north of Ashby Gap where US-50 crosses the AT west of Paris, VA

MAP: PATC Map 8; 0.2 mile to AT by connector trail

BUNKS & BEDS: 2 double-deck bunks in main room, plus mattresses for 8 in sleeping loft; total of 12 mattresses and blankets

COOKING: Fire pit outdoors and wood-burning cook stove in cabin

HEAT: Wood stove and fireplace

OUTSIDE FIRE: In established fire pit only

WATER: Dip from the creek located 100 yards back along access trail or use spring located 60 yards further down the blue-blazed trail starting near front steps

TOILET: Outhouse

ELECTRICITY: No

PETS: Yes

PATC Member-Only Cabin

Myron Glaser Cabin

Located on the western slope of the Blue Ridge, in Clarke County, Virginia, this stone cabin is a memorial to Myron Glaser, a long-time member of PATC and the travel writer for the *Washington Daily News*. The cabin site is a side benefit of the PATC Shelter, Cabins, and Cabin Lands Fund's purchase of a major parcel of land that was used to relocate the AT off roads that had been used for over a decade.

The Myron Glaser cabin has a sleeping loft that covers part of the main room (similar to the arrangement in the Jones Mountain and Hermitage cabins). It has skylights that greatly increase the amount of light inside and a large front porch that looks out to the southwest. The cabin is insulated and contains a large fireplace, as well as a fine wood-burning stove, making the cabin an excellent choice for winter camping. Access to the cabin is via the AT and a well-marked side trail.

Getting there: The cabin parking area, with room for about 12 cars, is the AT parking area on VA-601, just off of US-50 at Ashby Gap. Hike-in is 1.9 miles from the parking area.

Attention: The stairway to the loft and the edge of the loft overlooking the main room can be dangerous for small children.

FIRST FLOOR

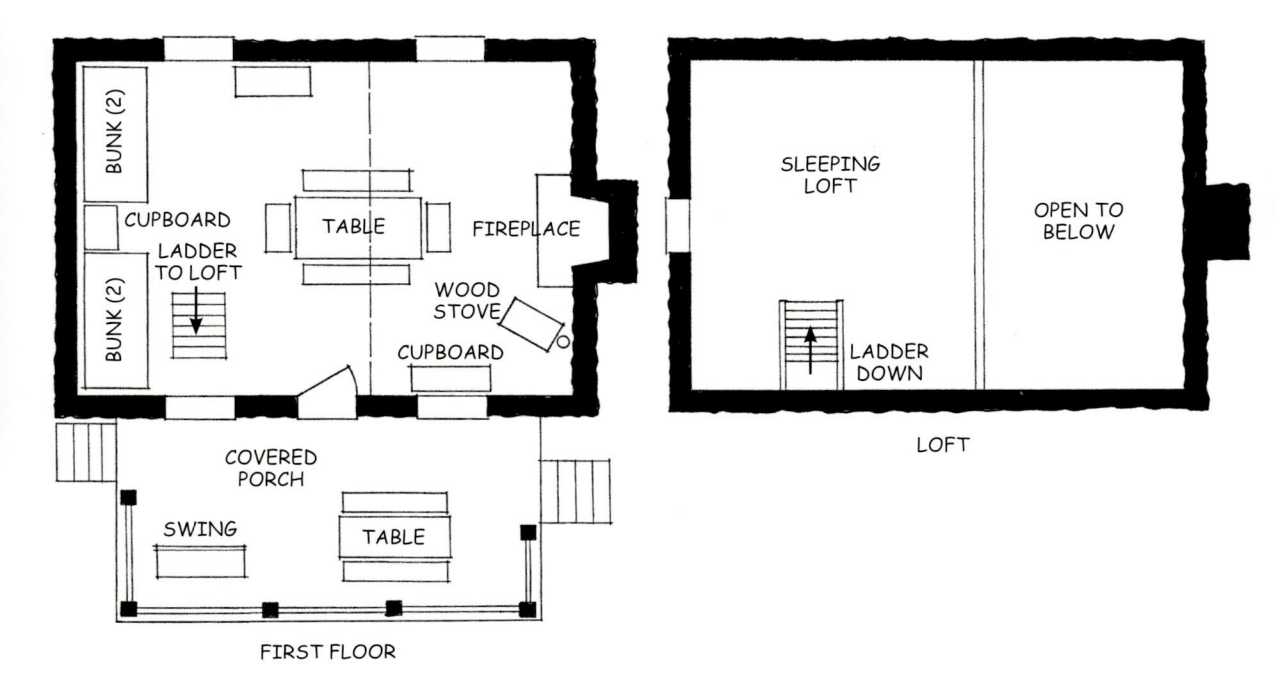

LOFT

Things to do: Hike along the AT via the access trail. See also PATC's "Appalachian Trail Guide to Maryland and Northern Virginia with Side Trails."

CABINS IN WEST VIRGINIA/NORTHERN VIRGINIA

CABIN TYPE: Primitive

CAPACITY: 4

LOCATION: Near ridges of Mill and Great North Mountains, George Washington National Forest, VA, about 8.5 miles northwest of Woodstock, VA

MAP: PATC Map F; cabin is not close to AT

BUNKS & BEDS: 2 double-deck, fold-down bunks with mats and blankets

COOKING: Wood stove; fire ring outside

HEAT: Wood stove

OUTSIDE FIRE: In fire pit only

WATER: Spring is about 500 feet south of the cabin, but may provide little water in very dry weather

TOILET: Outhouse

ELECTRICITY: No

PETS: Yes

Sugar Knob Cabin

Sugar Knob Cabin is an old stone cabin originally built for Forest Ranger use around 1920. If you like being off in the woods and enjoy being self-sufficient, then Sugar Knob is for you. Many are the log book entries of folks who fell in love with the cabin and its remoteness. Sugar Knob is the smallest of the PATC cabins at ten square feet. It is located on the Virginia/West Virginia border at an altitude of 3,000 feet near the ridge of Mill Mountain, in the Great North Mountain area of George Washington National Forest. This is the consummate backpackers' sanctuary. Competence in backcountry hiking skills is needed as approach trails involve steep climbing. Be prepared for harsh weather late fall through early spring. Despite the long driving distance and the strenuous hike-in, Sugar Knob is well worth the effort and presents an experience which will evoke many fond memories.

    Getting there: The roads to the cabin are west of the Woodstock exit on I-81. After several miles, the roads are gravel forest roads that go to the parking area after crossing Little Stony Creek. The hike-in is 3.2 miles uphill on the Little Stony Creek Trail. Be aware, though, that the Little Stony Creek trailhead off of the forest service road is closed via a locked gate from the first weekend in February till the first weekend in April. If the gate on the forest road is closed, then go to the Wolf Gap Recreation Area campground trailhead, where there is parking for ten cars. If you park there, the hike-in is 6.7 miles. There are also other alternative hike-in locations via the Trout Valley and Halfmoon Peak Trail, or the Tuscarora Trail from the traihead south of the community of Zepp.

    Attention: For the latest information about forest road closures, call the Forest Service at 540-984-4101.

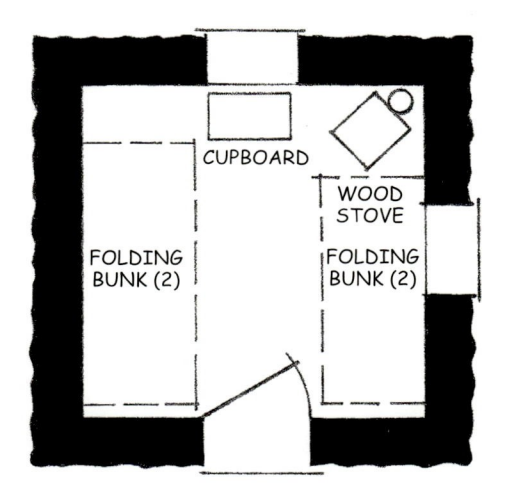

Things to do: Several other approach hikes are feasible from other trailheads, such as Halfmoon Trail or Tuscarora/Pond Run Trail (eight stream crossings). There are nice views along Mill Mountain Trail and possible side trip to the view at Big Schloss. Consult PATC's "Circuit Hikes in Virginia, West Virginia, Maryland, and Pennsylvania," and "The Tuscarora Trail, South" trail guides, or "Guide to Great North Mountain Trails."

CABINS IN WEST VIRGINIA/NORTHERN VIRGINIA

CABIN TYPE: Modern

CAPACITY: 8

LOCATION: North end of Fort Valley of the Massanutten, west of Front Royal, VA

MAP: PATC Map G; cabin is not close to AT

BUNKS & BEDS: 3 double-deck bunks, 2 bunks, with mattresses for each bunk

COOKING: Electric stove and oven, sink, and refrigerator; outside grill

HEAT: Wood stove

OUTSIDE FIRE: Not allowed

WATER: Hot and cold running well water; but renters should bring their own drinking water

TOILET: 1 bathroom with sink, toilet, and bathtub/shower

ELECTRICITY: Yes

PETS: Yes

PATC Member-Only Cabin

Glass House Cabin

PATC member and noted geologist Jewell Glass willed her Fort Valley house to the club upon her death in 1966. The Glass House is small but well-equipped. It is located in the valley created by the Massanutten Mountains in the Shenandoah Valley of Virginia. It is a square stone building and has a screened porch with a view of the east ridge of the Massanutten Mountains all the way down to Kennedy Peak. The cabin is located on an unusual "shale barren" formation that contains interesting and rare plants, some introduced by Miss Glass, a one-time U.S. government geologist. Glass House offers great hiking in the Elizabeth Furnace area.

Getting there: The cabin is near the Elizabeth Furnace Recreation Area and the driveway is reachable via paved state roads. The gated gravel driveway is steep. Use care, especially in snow and ice. There is parking for four cars at the top of the driveway. There is no hike-in unless bad weather prevents ascending the driveway. In that case, park off the pavement at the bottom of hill, where there is space for two cars, and hike uphill about 100 yards to the cabin.

Attention: Do not bring or use electric heating, as the wiring is inadequate for this use.

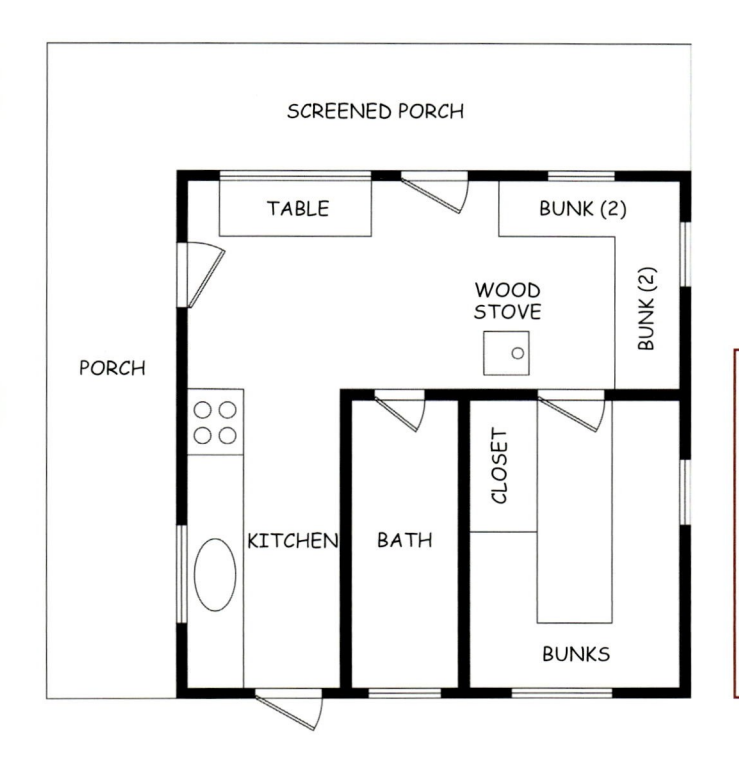

Things to do: Hike the extensive trail system in the Elizabeth Furnace area. Trails include portions of the Tuscarora and Massanutten Trails. A strong hiker can get to Signal Knob and its view of the Shenandoah Valley from the cabin. Passage Creek has fishing and canoeing. See also PATC's "Guide to Massanutten Mountain."

CABINS IN WEST VIRGINIA/NORTHERN VIRGINIA   55

CABIN TYPE: Modern

CAPACITY: 6

LOCATION: East side of the north section of SNP, near the town of "Little" Washington, VA

MAP: PATC Map 9; more than 4 miles to AT by various trails

BUNKS & BEDS: 1 double platform bed with a short ladder, 1 double futon, and 1 double-deck bunk with 2 mattresses

COOKING: Electric stove/oven for cooking; mini-fridge;

HEAT: Wood stove and electric baseboard heat

OUTSIDE FIRE: In fire ring only

WATER: Well water from tap is safe to drink

TOILET: Indoor bathroom with sink, toilet, and shower

ELECTRICITY: Yes

PETS: No

PATC Member-Only Cabin

Horwitz Cabin

Horwitz is one of the jewels of the PATC cabin system. Like Glass House and Cliff's House, it is one-room, cozy, and modern. The cabin is located within three miles of the town of Washington, Virginia and adjoins Shenandoah National Park. The driveway snakes up a small mountain to a secluded area overlooking a pond and mountains in the distance—a perfect getaway cabin for hikers or those who want to explore the attractions in Rappahannock County.

The late Dr. Norman Horwitz, a prominent neurosurgeon, and his wife Elinor Horwitz, a writer, both active hikers and birders, bought this land in 1973 "in a fit of passion." They built the cabin as a do-it-yourself project. Two months of weekends later, with the help of family and friends, they finished it, and decades later a contractor added two more sections to the structure, a larger front porch, and indoor plumbing and electricity.

Getting there: Renters can drive to this cabin; there is no hike-in. Most of the way is paved road, but the last mile is dirt, VA-625/Mount Marshall Road. The property's driveway is about 0.5 mile and the last part is steep. In snowy or icy weather, it might be necessary to park on the road and walk up the driveway. Along the driveway and near the cabin, there is room for about six cars to park.

Attention: This area is frequented by black bears, so keep food and trash inside the cabin or car. The double bed is elevated and may be difficult for some to climb up to or easy to roll out of. While the PATC property is 32 acres, the cabin is near an adjoining residence which can be seen in the winter when the leaves are off the trees.

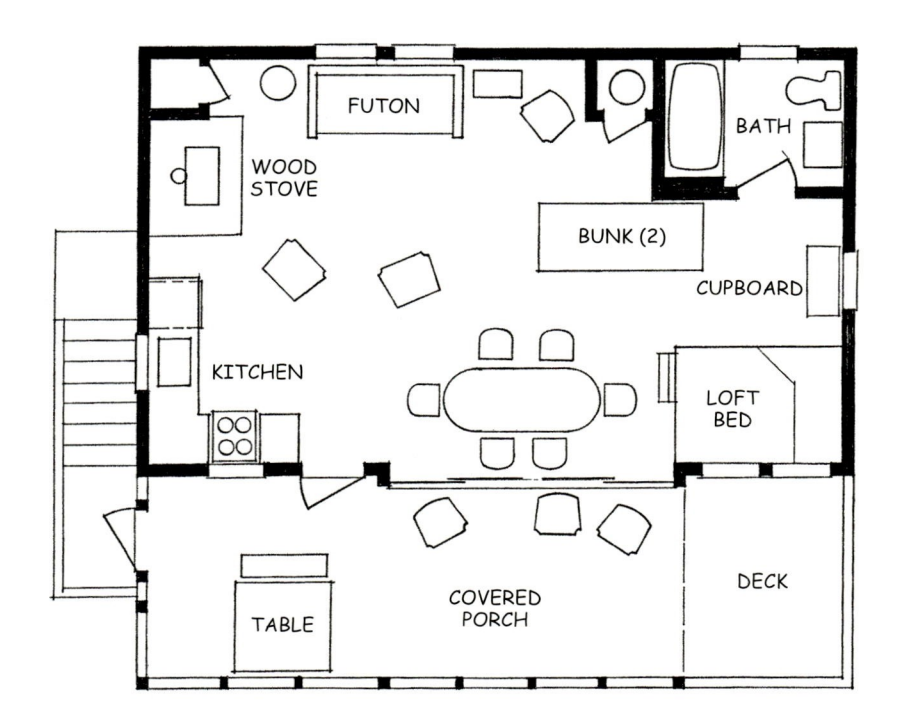

Things to do: The cabin adjoins the Mount Marshall Trail that goes into SNP and connects to the park's trail system. Visitors can drive to other trailheads nearby or into the Park and hike from Skyline Drive. See also PATC's "Circuit Hikes in Shenandoah National Park" or "Appalachian Trail Guide to Shenandoah National Park with Side Trails."

CABINS IN WEST VIRGINIA/NORTHERN VIRGINIA

CABIN TYPE: Primitive

CAPACITY: 8

LOCATION: In North District of SNP, near Elk Wallow Wayside and Matthews Arm Campground on Skyline Drive

MAP: PATC Map 9; 0.1 mile to AT by connector trail

BUNKS & BEDS: 4 double-deck bunks and 8 mattresses

COOKING: Wood stove, outside fireplace under eaves

HEAT: Wood stove

OUTSIDE FIRE: In outside fireplace only

WATER: Spring 130 feet southeast of cabin

TOILET: Outhouse

ELECTRICITY: No

PETS: Yes

Range View Cabin

This cabin is a one-room stone structure in the Northern Section of Shenandoah National Park (SNP). It was built by PATC in 1933, but the title went to SNP when the park was established. The Club operates it, as it does five other cabins in the park, as a concessionaire. The cabin looks out on a cleared grassy area with a view of the valley on the eastern slopes of the Blue Ridge and top of Old Rag Mountain in the distance.

The cabin is on the docket to be listed in the National Register of Historic Buildings. The proximity of the AT and the park's Matthews Arm Campground may result in unexpected visitors, especially on weekends, but passing herds of deer make it a charming, cozy cabin for families with children.

Getting there: Parking for the cabin is at the Piney River Ranger Station on Skyline Drive, which is north of the SNP Thornton Gap Entrance at US-211. There is space for at least 20 cars. The hike-in, gently downhill, is 0.9 mile. If Skyline Drive is closed, a 6-mile hike up the mountain to the AT from the Piney Branch Trailhead at the end of VA-600 is required. The side trail east of the AT to the cabin is 0.1 mile.

Attention: Skyline Drive may close during snowfall, icy conditions, emergencies, and hunting season. Before leaving home, call SNP at 540-999-3500 regarding road closures. Be prepared to pay the Park entrance fee. During hunting season (mid-November to early January), the entrance gates close from 5:00 pm to 8:00 am.

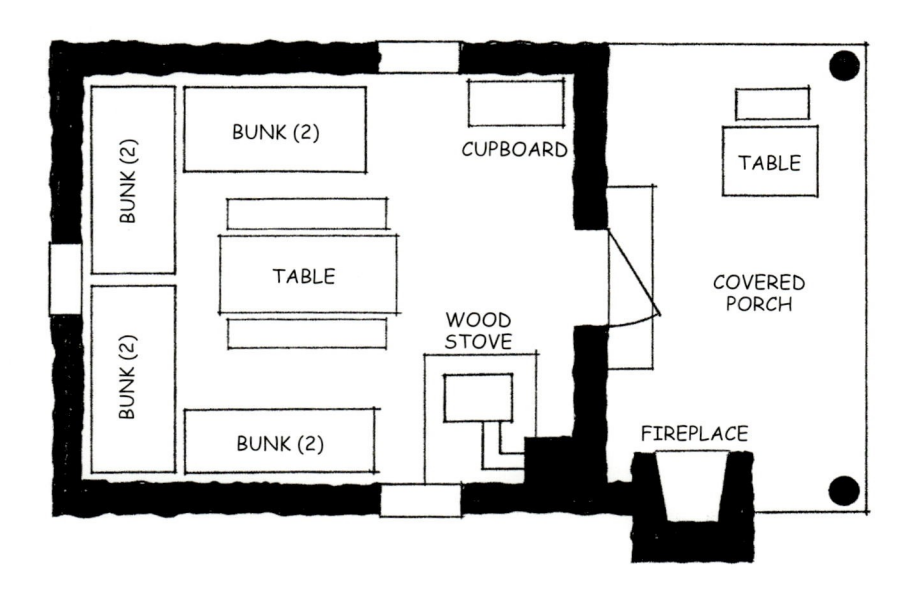

Things to do: *Hike in the Elkwallow and Matthews Arm areas and along Piney Ridge, Piney Branch, and the AT. Consult PATC's "Circuit Hikes in Shenandoah National Park" or "Appalachian Trail Guide to Shenandoah National Park and Side Trails." Attend Ranger talks and hikes in summer.*

CABINS IN AND NEAR SHENANDOAH NATIONAL PARK, VIRGINIA 59

CABIN TYPE: Modern

CAPACITY: 11

LOCATION: Shaver Hollow, just outside the western border of SNP, near Luray, VA

MAP: PATC Map 10; 2.9 miles to AT by trail

BUNKS & BEDS: 1 double bed with mattress in each of 2 upstairs bedrooms; 6 bunk beds with foam mats and blankets in the bunkroom

COOKING: Modern kitchen with electric cook stove and refrigerator

HEAT: Wood-burning heating stove; fireplace with insert; electric baseboard heat in the kitchen/eating area (heat is pre-set and must not be adjusted)

OUTSIDE FIRE: Not allowed

WATER: Potable pumped well water provides hot and cold running water in kitchen and bathroom

TOILET: Bathroom with sink, toilet, and bathtub; no shower; outhouse

ELECTRICITY: Yes

PETS: Yes

PATC Member-Only Cabin

Lambert Cabin

Lambert Cabin was the home of Eileen and Darwin Lambert for more than 40 years. Darwin Lambert was a long-time PATC member, conservationist, author, editor, and the first employee of SNP. The log structure was built prior to the American Civil War, and the "back end" or kitchen/dining room area was added before 1900. Darwin passed away in February of 2007, but his words and ideas live on:

"We've done a lot for this place; the soil is more fertile now; the life is more abundant and diverse. Yet the place has done more for us than we've done for it. This land is interwoven with us, with our spirits, bodies, minds, and emotions....We share glorious days and nights with birds and frogs, deer and foxes and bears, as well as with other humans, and with trees and the winds that rustle the leaves or sway the branches, and the creek that girgles [sic] in its channel among boulders and carries life in many forms. Here we talk with Earth, are partners with Earth, creating together. We try to learn Earth's ways...and harmonize ours with them—and discuss and create also with human friends and institutions to keep learning humanities ways and willingness's—to help toward fuller harmony, continuing our social membership without losing our citizenship in Earth."

Getting there: Access to the cabin is via paved, gravel, and dirt roads off of US-211 after it crosses Skyline Drive heading west. The road to Lambert Cabin is a rough old mountain road but is passable to automobiles. The entire road is on private property so please be respectful of other people's property and their continued support of PATC. There is parking for four cars by the cabin.

Attention: The ceiling beams in most of the rooms are low so renters over 5' 10" will need to be extremely careful not to bump their heads.

STORAGE

KITCHEN

DINING

SITTING

STAIR UP

GAME ROOM

FIREPLACE

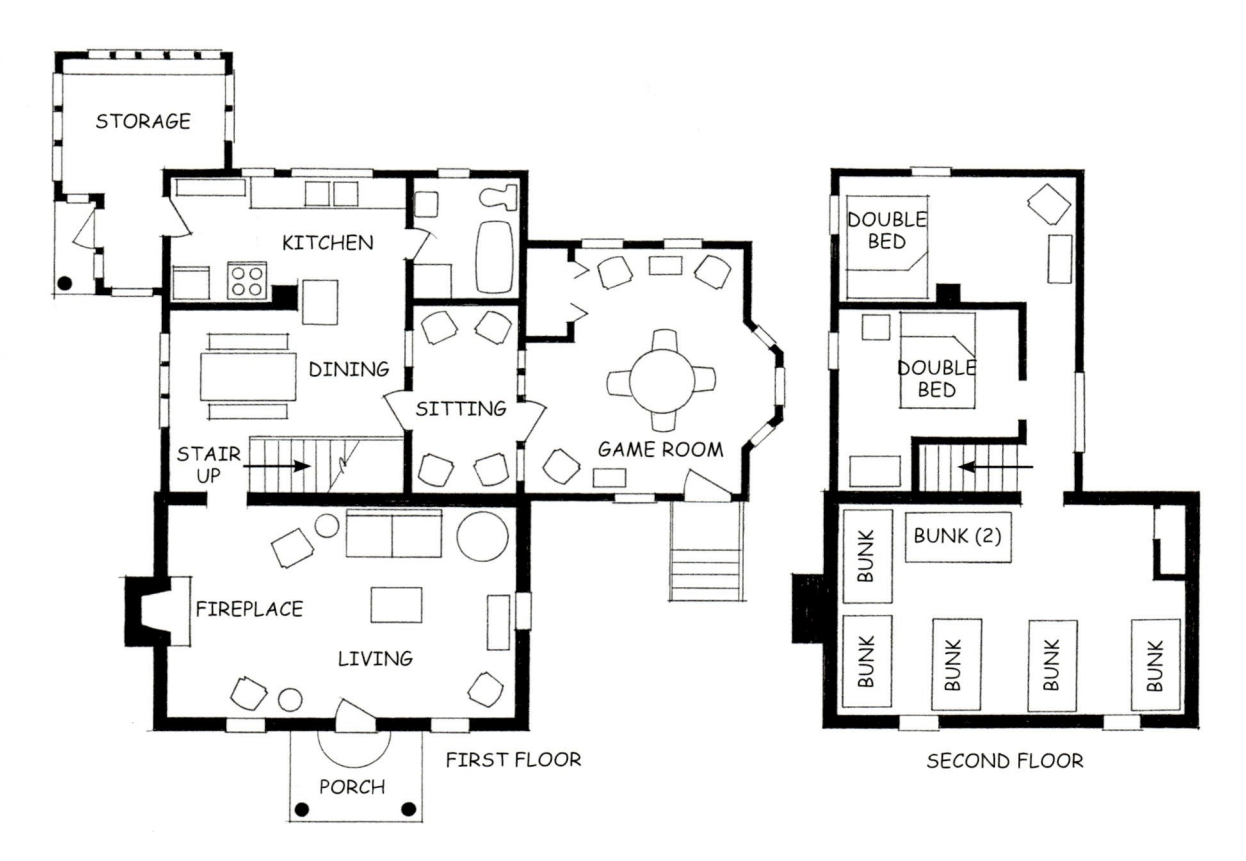

LIVING

PORCH

FIRST FLOOR

DOUBLE BED

DOUBLE BED

BUNK

BUNK (2)

BUNK

BUNK

BUNK

BUNK

SECOND FLOOR

Things to do: *Explore the grounds; hike up the steep Crushers Ridge Trail to the AT and over to Nicholson Hollow.*

CABINS IN AND NEAR SHENANDOAH NATIONAL PARK, VIRGINIA 61

CABIN TYPE: Primitive

CAPACITY: 8

LOCATION: Shaver Hollow, just outside the western border of SNP, near Luray, VA

MAP: PATC Map 10; 2+ miles to AT by trail

BUNKS & BEDS: 2 double bunks, 2 double-width bunks in loft

COOKING: Wood heat stove and in fireplace; outdoor stone grill

HEAT: Wood stove and fireplace

OUTSIDE FIRE: In grill only

WATER: Spring about 75 yards away

TOILET: Outhouse

ELECTRICITY: No

PETS: Yes

PATC Member-Only Cabin

Tulip Tree Cabin

Tulip Tree Cabin is located in Shaver Hollow on land donated to the PATC by Darwin and Eileen Lambert. The Lamberts were long-time PATC members and conservationists, authors, editors, and philosophers. The cabin was designed by PATC Honorary Life Member Charlie Graf and built by a crew of volunteers under his leadership. It was built from the ground up using native materials and primitive hand tools much as our pioneer forefathers would have done. All of the furniture except four chairs was hand crafted by volunteers, including the beautiful pie safe, which is an exact copy of one owned by the crew chief's grandmother. Construction of the cabin took more than eight years.

The cabin is a little larger and fancier than the average pioneer mountain cabin. It is bright, cheerful, and airy in the summer. When closed up in the winter, it is nice and tight and can be kept toasty warm with the wood burning stove. There is also a fireplace. It is ideal for families with children.

Getting there: Access to the cabin is via paved, gravel, and dirt roads off of US-211 after it crosses Skyline Drive heading west. The dirt road to Tulip Tree Cabin is a rough old mountain road but is passable to automobiles. Drive slowly and expect a bumpy ride. The entire road is on private property so please be respectful of the property owners to ensure their continued goodwill toward PATC. There is space for two cars in the parking area, which is about 300 yards from the cabin.

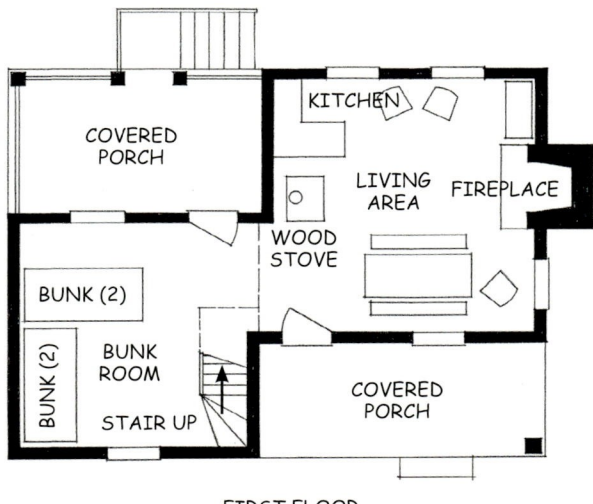

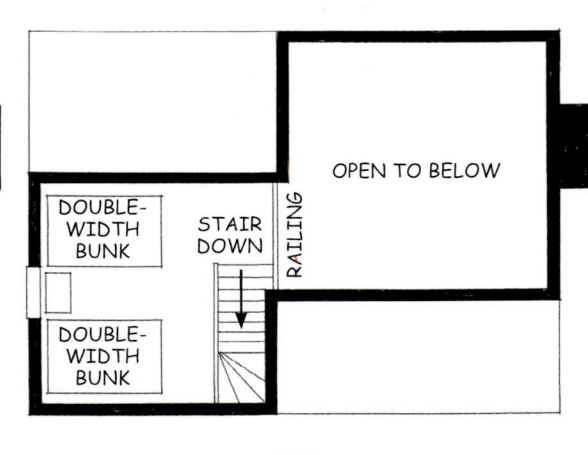

FIRST FLOOR

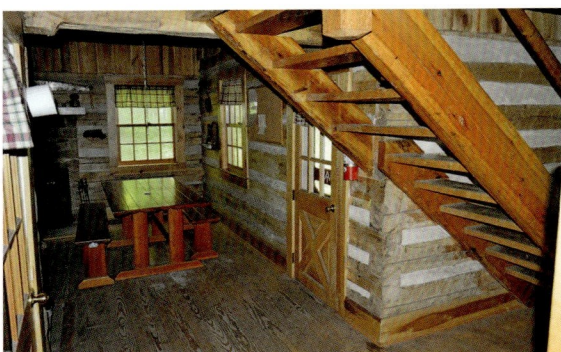

LOFT

Things to do: *Hike up to the AT on the Crusher Ridge Trail and then possibly down to Corbin Cabin on the Nicholson Hollow Trail (a strenuous 9 mile round trip) or go either direction on the AT. Drive up to SNP and Skyline Drive.*

CABINS IN AND NEAR SHENANDOAH NATIONAL PARK, VIRGINIA

CABIN TYPE: Modern

CAPACITY: 6

LOCATION: East of Luray, VA on the western side of SNP next to PATC's Lambert Tract

MAP: PATC Map 10; 2+ miles to AT by trail

BUNKS & BEDS: Loft bedroom with double bed and 1 double-deck bunk; bedroom with double bed downstairs

COOKING: Electric stove/oven, refrigerator, dishwasher, microwave, toaster, and coffee maker

HEAT: Electric heating, indoor fireplace, fan for summer

OUTSIDE FIRE: In grill or fire ring only

WATER: Potable well water from tap

TOILET: 2 indoor bathrooms with sink, toilet, and shower

ELECTRICITY: Yes

PETS: No

PATC Member-Only Cabin

Huntley Cabin

The Huntley Cabin is a two-story, fully furnished house located just outside of Luray, Virginia. The cabin sits next to a babbling brook on 100 acres in Tutweiler Hollow on the western side of SNP next to PATC's Lambert Tract. It was built by the Huntley family of Bethesda, Maryland in 1979 as a mountain getaway on the site of an old mountain homestead. Mrs. Huntley so appreciated art that she built a bridge over the stream near the cabin that is a copy of a bridge in Claude Monet's garden in France, which he used in many of his paintings. The cabin has both a front porch for sitting and a screened porch on the back for outdoor meals. It is a good cabin for families with children.

Getting there: Access to the cabin is via paved, gravel, and dirt roads off of US-211 after it crosses Skyline Drive heading west. The road to Huntley Cabin is a rough old mountain road but is passable to automobiles. Drive slowly and expect a bumpy ride. The first part of the road is on private property. Please be respectful of the property owners to ensure their continued goodwill toward PATC. There is parking for three to four cars by the cabin.

Attention: This area is frequented by black bears so never leave food or trash unattended outside, on the porch, or around the cabin. Keep food and trash inside the cabin or car.

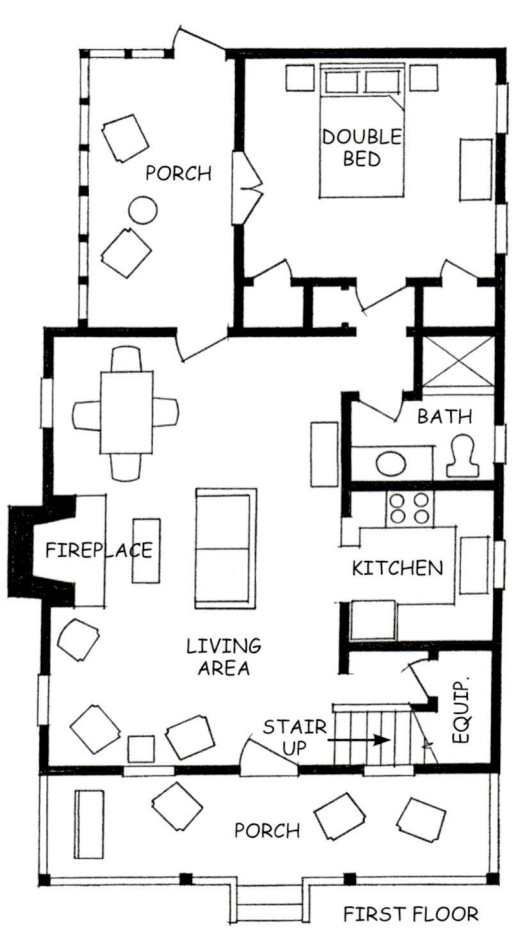

Things to do: *Follow the old mountain road that leads from Jewell Hollow Road and straight past the pond (instead of turning left to reach the driveway to Huntley) up to the Crusher Ridge Trail and follow it 2+ miles to the AT.*

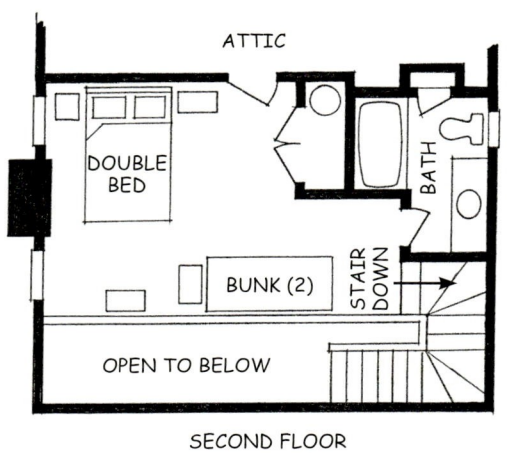

FIRST FLOOR

SECOND FLOOR

CABINS IN AND NEAR SHENANDOAH NATIONAL PARK, VIRGINIA 65

CABIN TYPE: Primitive

CAPACITY: 12

LOCATION: 6.3 miles south of Thornton Gap, off of Skyline Drive in Central District of SNP

MAP: PATC map 10; 1.5 miles to AT by connector trail

BUNKS & BEDS: 1 double-width bunk and 2 double-deck bunks in annex; sleeping loft in cabin

COOKING: Wood stove

HEATING: Fireplace in living room, wood stove in kitchen

WATER: 130 feet to the Hughes River, which is reliable year-round

TOILET: Outhouse

ELECTRICITY: No

PETS: Yes

Corbin Cabin

Corbin Cabin is nestled in a lovely area beside the Hughes River in SNP's Nicholson Hollow. It is a two-story solid chestnut log cabin and was the mountain home of George Corbin, the primary supplier of moonshine to Skyland. It was restored by PATC labor in 1953–54 and has been kept as close to original condition as possible. It is on the National Register of Historic Places, which limits the enhancements that can be made to it. The cabin is highly visible to hikers on surrounding trails. In very cold weather, it takes a lot of wood to adequately heat the cabin.

Getting there: The trailhead for the Corbin Cabin Cutoff Trail is located at the Skyline Drive parking area past Mile Marker 37. This fairly steep trail winds down the mountainside 1.4 miles where you must cross a stream, the headwaters of the Hughes River. Normally, large boulders and stones provide a dry crossing; however, after an extremely heavy rain, the water can be higher.

When Skyline Drive is closed, a 4.3 mile hike-in from the Old Rag parking lot is required. Hike 0.5 mile up the road to the Nicholson Hollow Trail trailhead and then hike 3.8 miles on the Nicholson Hollow Trail to the cabin. Several river crossings with stepping stones will occur, all very shallow during normal water conditions.

Attention: Skyline Drive may close during snowfall, icy conditions, emergencies, and hunting season. Before leaving home, call SNP at 540-999-3500 regarding road closures. Be prepared to pay the Park entrance fee. During hunting season (mid-November to early January), the entrance gates close from 5:00 pm to 8:00 am. This cabin is not recommended for families with small children because of the strenuous hike in and out.

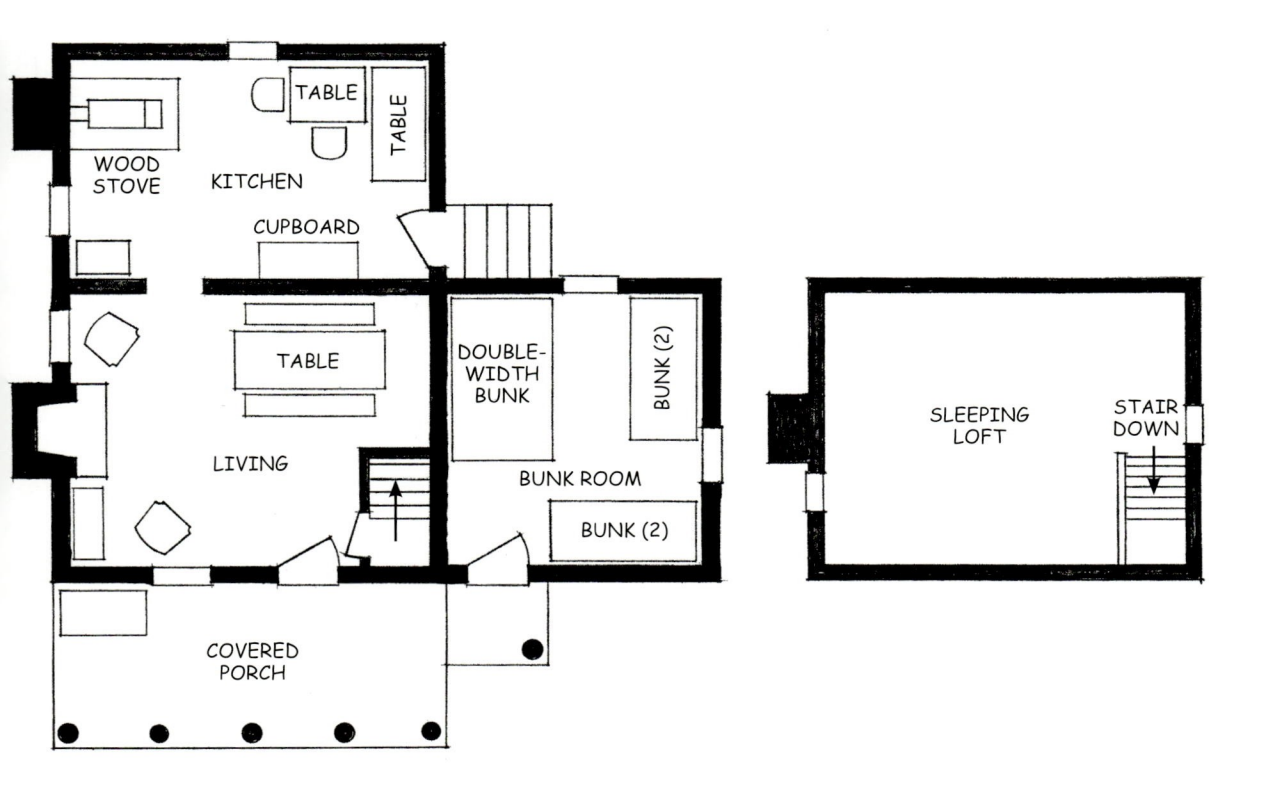

Things to do: This cabin affords many opportunities for hikes, some of them circuits, along Nicholson Hollow, Corbin Cabin Cutoff, Indian Run, and Hannah Run Trails to name a few. It is a short but strenuous hike up to the summit of Robertson Mountain for a view towards Old Rag Mountain. There are old cabin sites that can be seen from the trail as well as places along the Hughes River for a cooling dip. Refer to PATC's "Circuit Hikes in Shenandoah National Park" and the "Appalachian Trail Guide to Shenandoah National Park with Side Trails."

CABINS IN AND NEAR SHENANDOAH NATIONAL PARK, VIRGINIA

CABIN TYPE: Modern

CAPACITY: 8

LOCATION: Just off the road/trail below Old Rag Mountain in Madison County, VA

MAP: PATC Map 10; 6 miles to AT by connector trail

BUNKS & BEDS: 1 queen bed in bedroom, 2 bunk beds in bunk area, 2 single daybeds main room

COOKING: Electric range, refrigerator

HEAT: Wood stove and electric baseboard

OUTSIDE FIRE: In outdoor fire ring only

WATER: Hot and cold potable running water from well

TOILET: Indoor bathroom with sink, toilet, and shower

ELECTRICITY: Yes

PETS: No

PATC Member-Only Cabin

Old Rag Cabin

This modern wheelchair-accessible cabin is adjacent to Shenandoah National Park near the base of Old Rag Mountain. The central structure was built in 1878 as a log cabin, which was relocated from rural Hancock, Maryland to the Virginia site. Construction of this cabin by PATC volunteer work crews began in 2012 with the demolition of the rundown structure on the site by the Cadillac Crew, after which the Lincoln Loggers work crew built a new foundation, disassembled, moved, and reassembled the log cabin, and also created a new addition. Major construction was completed in 2016 with the majority of the work performed by the Lincoln Loggers.

The log cabin portion contains a first-floor living space and a second-story loft and bedroom, with the addition containing a full kitchen and bathroom. Additional features are a large screened-in porch and very spacious deck, situated on a spring-fed brook. This is the perfect cabin for those interested in hiking Old Rag and Robertson Mountain trails.

Getting there: The cabin is 0.3 mile past the Shenandoah National Park Old Rag Parking Lot and trailhead in Nethers, Virginia. Nethers is about 11 miles south of Sperryville. There is parking for three to four cars by the cabin.

Attention: This area is frequented by black bears. Never leave human food, pet food, or trash unattended outside, either on the porch or around the cabin. Keep food and trash inside the cabin or in your car. Do not trespass on adjacent private property.

FIRST FLOOR

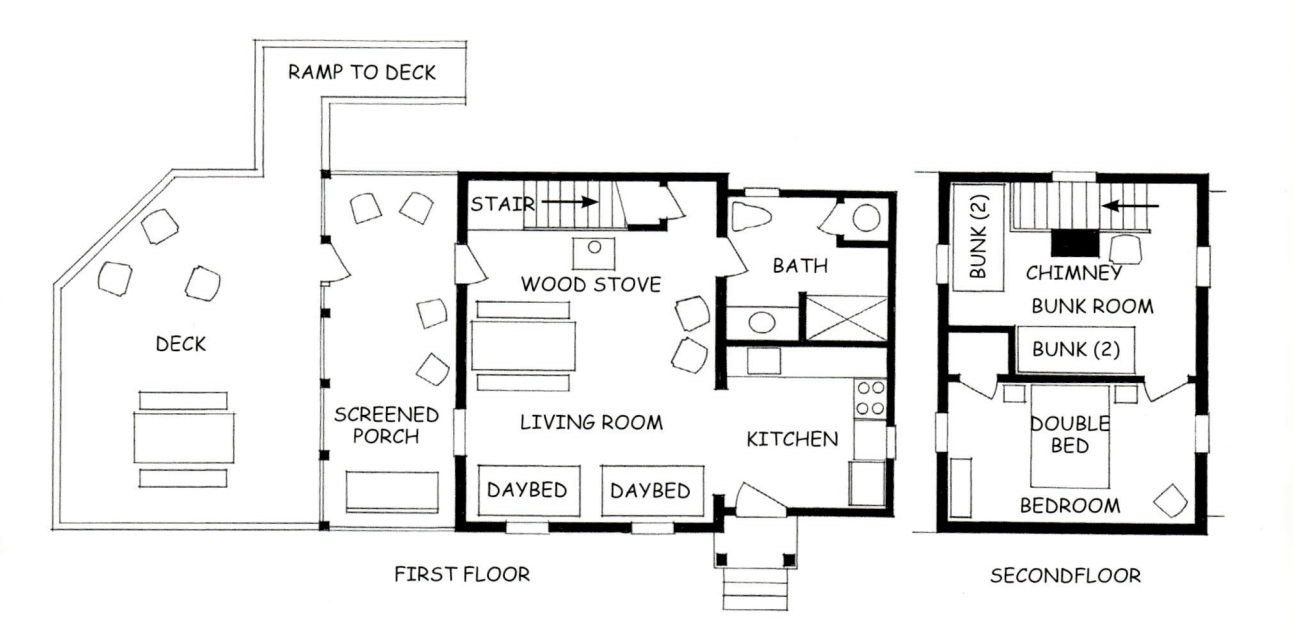

- RAMP TO DECK
- DECK
- SCREENED PORCH
- STAIR
- WOOD STOVE
- LIVING ROOM
- DAYBED
- DAYBED
- BATH
- KITCHEN

SECOND FLOOR

- BUNK (2)
- CHIMNEY
- BUNK ROOM
- BUNK (2)
- DOUBLE BED
- BEDROOM

Things to do: The Old Rag and Robertson Mountain trailheads are a half mile further up Nethers Road and there are numerous less strenuous trails in the area. See also PATC's "Circuit Hikes in Shenandoah National Park" and "Appalachian Trail Guide to Shenandoah National Park with Side Trails."

CABINS IN AND NEAR SHENANDOAH NATIONAL PARK, VIRGINIA 69

CABIN TYPE: Primitive

CAPACITY: 8

LOCATION: Central Section of SNP on the western slope of Hawksbill Mountain, 16 miles south of Thornton Gap, 2 miles north of Big Meadows

MAP: PATC Map 10; 0.2 mile to AT by connector trail

BUNKS & BEDS: 2 double-width, double-deck bunks

COOKING: Wood stove, outside fireplace on covered porch

HEAT: Wood stove

OUTSIDE FIRE: Only in outside fireplace; firewood is in short supply as site is shared with AT hut

WATER: Rock Spring is 50 yards north of cabin

TOILET: Outhouse

ELECTRICITY: No

PETS: Yes

Rock Spring Cabin

Rock Spring is on the western slope of Hawksbill Mountain in the Central District in SNP. It looks out across Page Valley to the Massanutten Range in what is described as the best view from any PATC cabin. In winter, the twinkling of the town of Stanley in the valley presents a living Christmas card scene. The cabin is exposed to the west wind and is very cold in winter, although the wood stove helps.

Built of squared logs by the park in 1936, with a stone floor, the cabin is proposed to be listed in The National Register of Historic Places. It has an outdoor fireplace under the overhanging porch roof, as well as a stove inside, both usable for cooking. The cabin makes a fine base for the Hawksbill Mountain hike. Hawksbill summit (4,049 feet) is the highest point of land in the park. The AT Rock Spring Shelter is very near the cabin so do not expect privacy.

Getting there: Normal access to the cabin is from Skyline Drive, 18 miles south of Thornton Gap (US-211). Parking area is near milepost 48, adjacent to the Spitler Knoll Overlook. Park at the designated cabin parking place where there is space for five cars. Hike-in is 0.6 mile on the AT and 0.2 mile on the side trail to the cabin. If Skyline Drive is closed, the hike-in is a challenging 5.8 miles uphill from the east valley via the Cedar Run Trail and AT.

Attention: Skyline Drive may close during snowfall, icy conditions, emergencies, and hunting season. Before leaving home, call SNP at 540-999-3500 regarding road closures. Be prepared to pay the Park entrance fee. During hunting season (mid-November to early January), the entrance gates close from 5:00 pm to 8:00 am.

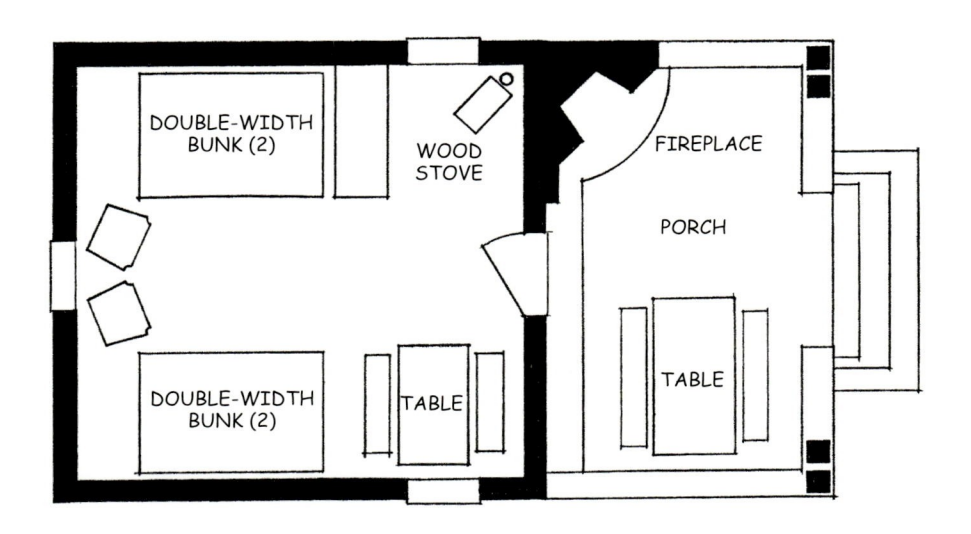

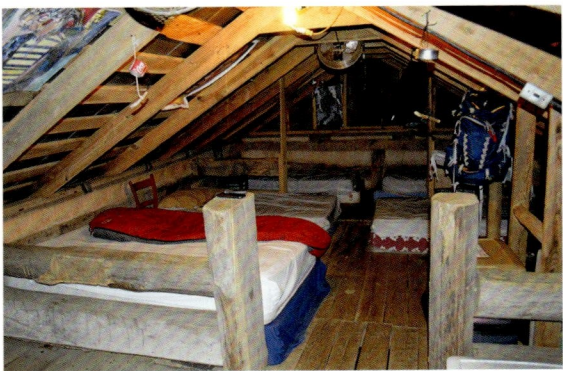

Things to do: Hike Hawksbill Mountain, the AT, and in Big Meadows; White Oak Canyon is a popular day hike; also see activities listed at other SNP cabins. See also PATC's "Circuit Hikes in Shenandoah National Park" and "Appalachian Trail Guide to Shenandoah National Park with Side Trails."

CABINS IN AND NEAR SHENANDOAH NATIONAL PARK, VIRGINIA

CABIN TYPE: Semi-primitive

CAPACITY: 12

LOCATION: East side of the Central District of SNP, at the headwaters of Strother Run, 2.5 miles west of Syria, VA

MAP: PATC Map 10; 6.0 miles to AT by trail

BUNKS & BEDS: 1 bunk, 1 double-deck bunk, and 1 double-width, double-deck bunk on first floor; 5 bunks on second floor

COOKING: Wood cook stove

HEAT: Wood stove in living room

OUTSIDE FIRE: Fire ring with grill

WATER: Spring 120 feet from cabin is not always reliable; recommend bringing supplemental water

TOILET: Outhouse

ELECTRICITY: Yes, lights only

PETS: Yes

PATC Member-Only Cabin

Meadows Cabin

Meadows Cabin is a chestnut log cabin built in 1913 by Edgar Meadows. The cabin stayed in the Meadows family until 1981, when PATC purchased the cabin and 94 acres. Abutting SNP, Meadows Cabin has excellent access to numerous hiking trails, among which are the Upper Dark Hollow Trail (a spur of the Rose River Trail System) and the Doubletop Ridge Trail, laid out by PATC member Charley Thomas in the late 1930s. The cabin is spacious with two rooms and a large kitchen downstairs and one large room upstairs. An efficient wood heating stove, in addition to a cook stove, makes Meadows a cozy place to stay in cold weather. The open spaces around the cabin give cabin users a delightful view of the Doubletop Ridge and the valley below.

Getting there: The drive to the cabin goes past Graves Mountain Lodge in Syria, Virginia. Unlock the gate to the cabin road and proceed to the parking area, which has space for about four cars. Do not try to drive beyond the parking area. Hike-in is 0.2 mile on the cabin road.

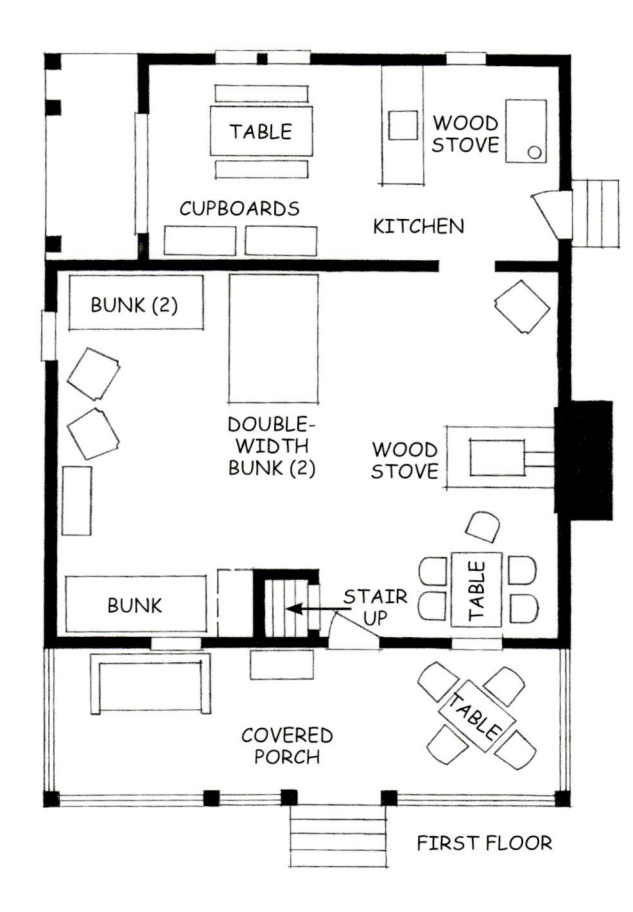

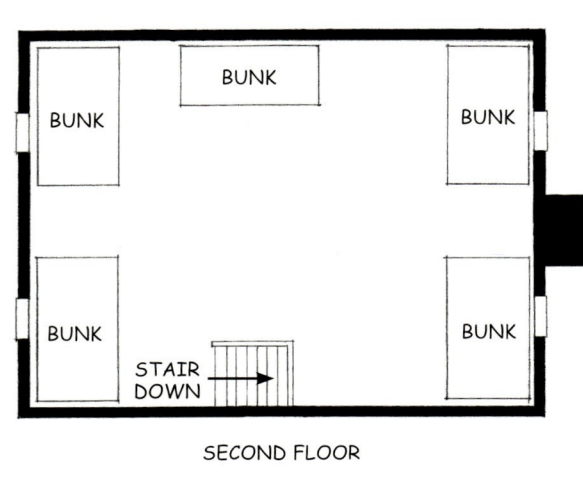

Things to do: Hike 1.1 mile trail on the Meadows property and the many trails in SNP; the old wagon road on site continues into SNP and offers excellent opportunity for cross-country skiing. See also PATC's "Appalachian Trail Guide to Shenandoah National Park with Side Trails."

CABINS IN AND NEAR SHENANDOAH NATIONAL PARK, VIRGINIA

CABIN TYPE: Modern

CAPACITY: 8

LOCATION: Elkton, VA west of SNP

MAP: PATC Map 10; no trail to AT; the Powell Mountain trailhead leading to AT is about 3.5 miles away

BUNKS & BEDS: 1 double-deck bunk and 1 double futon upstairs, 2 double-deck bunks downstairs

COOKING: Electric range and full size refrigerator with freezer

HEAT: Wood stove, electric baseboard heater in bathroom, electric heater for use in cold weather in downstairs area only

OUTSIDE FIRE: In charcoal grill only

WATER: Pumped spring water and electric water heater

TOILET: Inside toilet, sink, and shower

ELECTRICITY: Yes

PETS: Yes

PATC Member-Only Cabin

Cliff's House Cabin

Clifford Firestone, a long-time PATC member, had this house built in 1978 to his own design on a 19-acre tract of land. The tract is one piece of a farm purchased by five Club members and divided so that each fronts on the West Branch of Naked Creek and extends to the SNP boundary. Both Cliff's House and Robert Humphrey Cabin are on this tract.

Cliff built his house with living space upstairs and a workshop area downstairs. The living area has large sliding glass doors and picture windows. There are sliding barn doors to cover the windows. The cabin is well insulated, and little heat is needed to keep it cozy.

The house is good for families with children because of its ease of access, modern amenities, proximity to Naked Creek, and interesting natural environment, which includes a frog pond. Please be aware though, that small children must be supervised as there are tall stairways to the decks and main entrances. Small children ought not sleep in upper bunks as there are no safety rails.

Getting there: Four miles north of Elkton, Virginia, take several state roads with the last 0.4 mile to the driveway gate on a gravel road. Unlock the gate and continue slowly up the steep driveway to the house, where there is parking for four cars.

Attention: Although the cabin will have an unusual amount of lady bugs from October to May, they present no health issue. They were introduced into the woods to attack and eat the wooly adelgid scale insect that is killing the hemlock pine trees. Just push the lady bugs back outside of the cabin.

MAIN LEVEL

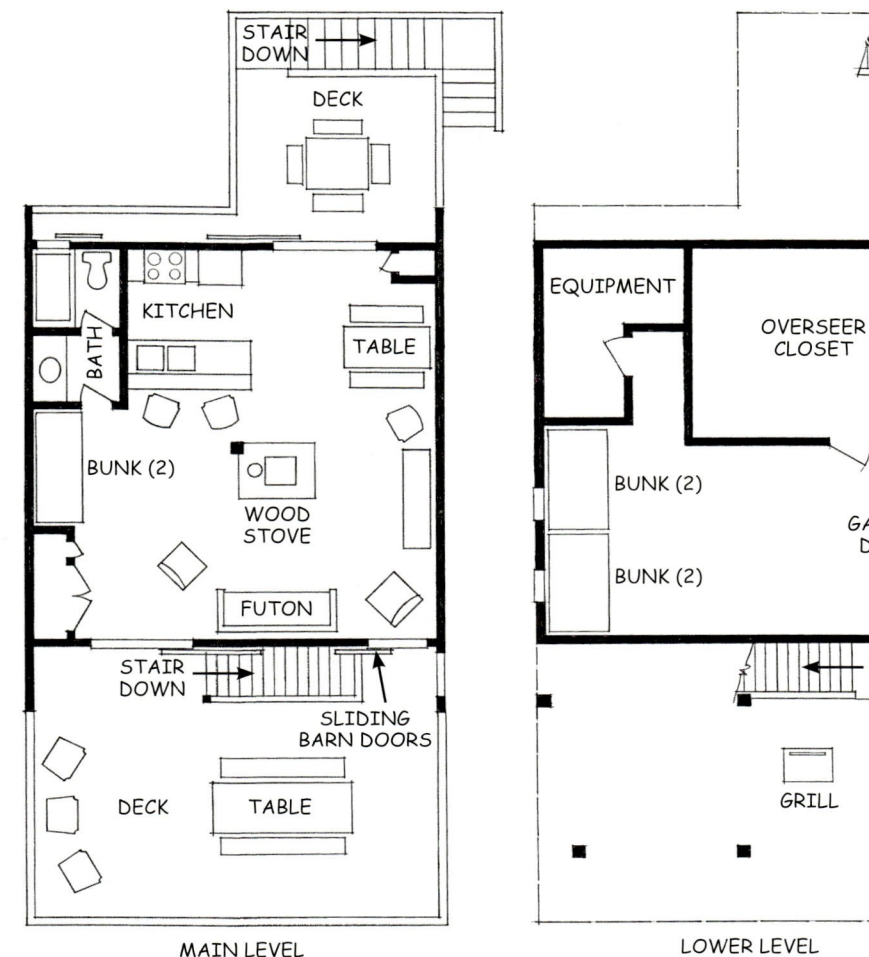

LOWER LEVEL

Things to do: Nearby hikes include Powell Mountain Trail and other trails in SNP. Trail behind Cliff's House goes to top of PATC land. Powell Mt. trailhead leading to the AT is about 3.5 miles away. See also PATC's "Circuit Hikes in Shenandoah National Park" and "Appalachian Trail Guide to Shenandoah National Park with Side Trails."

CABINS IN AND NEAR SHENANDOAH NATIONAL PARK, VIRGINIA   75

CABIN TYPE: Semi-primitive

CAPACITY: 8

LOCATION: Elkton, VA west of SNP

MAP: PATC Map 10; no trail to AT; the Powell Mountain trailhead leading to AT is about 3.5 miles away

BUNKS & BEDS: 2 double-deck bunks downstairs, 4 bunks upstairs

COOKING: Electric stove and refrigerator

HEAT: Wood stove

OUTSIDE FIRE: Fire pit and stone-built charcoal barbeque available

WATER: From spring through fall, spring water available at sink on porch; in winter, water is obtained from a spring located uphill from cabin; water can also be obtained from outdoor faucet on west side of Cliff's House

TOILET: Outhouse

ELECTRICITY: Yes

PETS: Yes

PATC Member-Only Cabin

Robert Humphrey Cabin

Robert Humphrey Cabin (formally called Weaver Cabin) is a two-story structure dedicated in 2011 and renamed for PATC Honorary Life member Robert Humphrey, who helped restore the cabin. Robert was a friend of PATC member Cliff Firestone whose house is now the Cliff's House Cabin that is situated on the hill above the Humphrey Cabin.

The Robert Humphrey Cabin was built 1780–1820. It was moved to this site and was the Joe Lam family homestead for more than 140 years. The cabin supports upstairs are made with tongue and groove junctions, put together with wooden pegs (no nails). The wood used to build the cabin was from the trees available on the property and included chestnut logs at the bottom, pine logs in the middle, and oak logs on the top rows. The different types are very evident by looking at the cabin from the front yard.

Getting there: The cabin is off of a state secondary road near the source of the West Branch of Naked Creek, northeast of Elkton, Virginia. Unlock the chain across the driveway to get to the cabin parking area on the left of the driveway. There is room for five cars in the flat gravel driveway parking area. There is no hike-in.

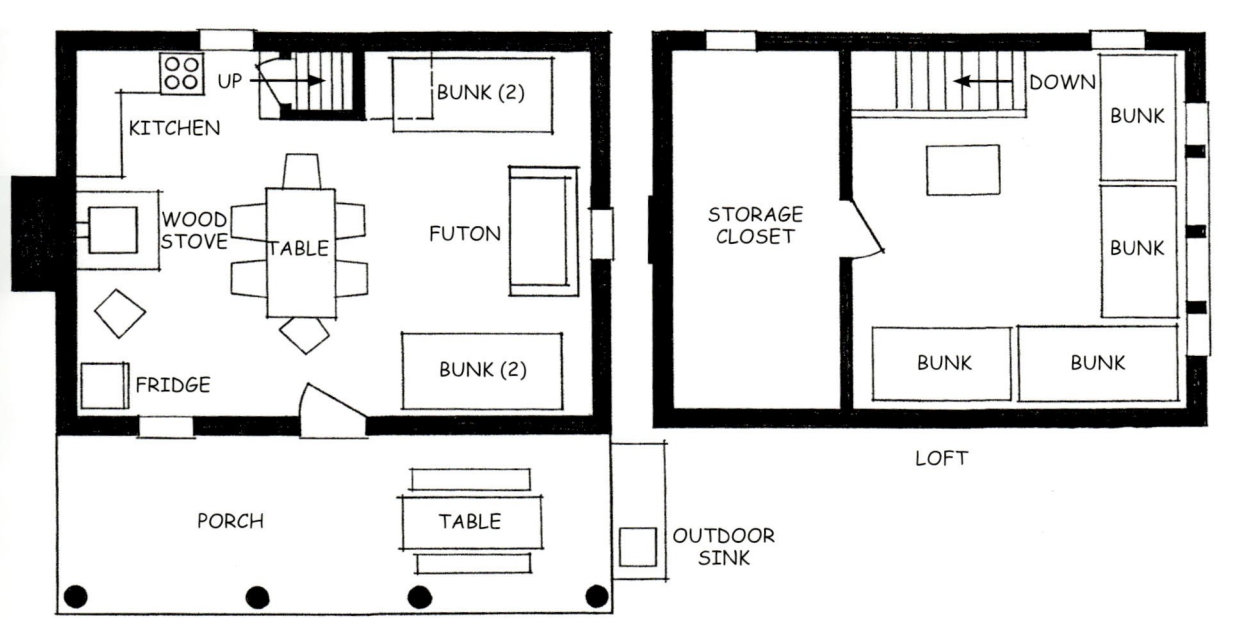

FIRST FLOOR

- KITCHEN
- UP
- BUNK (2)
- WOOD STOVE
- TABLE
- FUTON
- FRIDGE
- BUNK (2)
- PORCH
- TABLE
- OUTDOOR SINK

LOFT

- DOWN
- BUNK
- STORAGE CLOSET
- BUNK
- BUNK
- BUNK

Things to do: *Nearby hikes include Powell Mountain Trail and other trails in SNP. Trail behind Cliff's House goes to top of PATC land. Spur trails leading to the AT are about two miles away. See also PATC's "Circuit Hikes in Shenandoah National Park."*

CABIN TYPE: Primitive

CAPACITY: 10

LOCATION: Eastern side of the Central Section of SNP, near Graves Mill, VA

MAP: PATC Map 10; 5.9 miles to AT by trail

BUNKS & BEDS: 2 bunks downstairs; 1 bunk and space for 7 mattresses in loft

COOKING: Inside fireplace with swinging arm

HEAT: Fireplace and wood-burning stove

OUTSIDE FIRE: Not allowed

WATER: Spring about 80 feet from the cabin; during the summer, it is advisable to carry in supplemental water

TOILET: Outhouse

ELECTRICITY: No

PETS: Yes

Jones Mountain Cabin

The historic Jones Mountain Cabin is in a remote corner of the central section of the SNP. Jones Mountain requires the longest and hardest hike-in of any PATC cabin, but rewards the visitor with seclusion, charm, and a good story. The cabin was built in 1918 by moonshiner Harvey Nichols, who constructed it on the remains of the burned out cabin built by his father around 1855. The chestnut timbers hewn by Harvey are still in place, as are the stone foundation and fireplace built by his father. Jones Mountain Cabin is proposed to be listed in the National Register of Historic Buildings.

The cabin was rehabilitated by the PATC between 1969 and 1974. The cabin is bright and airy thanks to skylights and south-facing windows. Intrepid visitors may search for the nearby grave of Harvey Nichol's wife.

Getting there: It is possible to hike to Jones Mountain Cabin from Skyline Drive, but the shortest way is from the east side of the park. The drive to the trailhead, where there is parking for about ten vehicles, is on a paved, state-maintained road. There are no major hills, but the last few miles of the trip are on a narrow, rural road. The hike from the trailhead to the cabin is 3.8 miles. The trail is rocky in many places, and there is an elevation gain of 1,400 feet. At first, the trail follows the Staunton River, but then turns away from the river and becomes steep.

Attention: No outside fires are allowed and firewood is subject to SNP regulations. The porch has a drop off that could be dangerous for small children. The nearby spring may not be reliable in dry months and the hike to other water would be long.

CABINS IN AND NEAR SHENANDOAH NATIONAL PARK, VIRGINIA

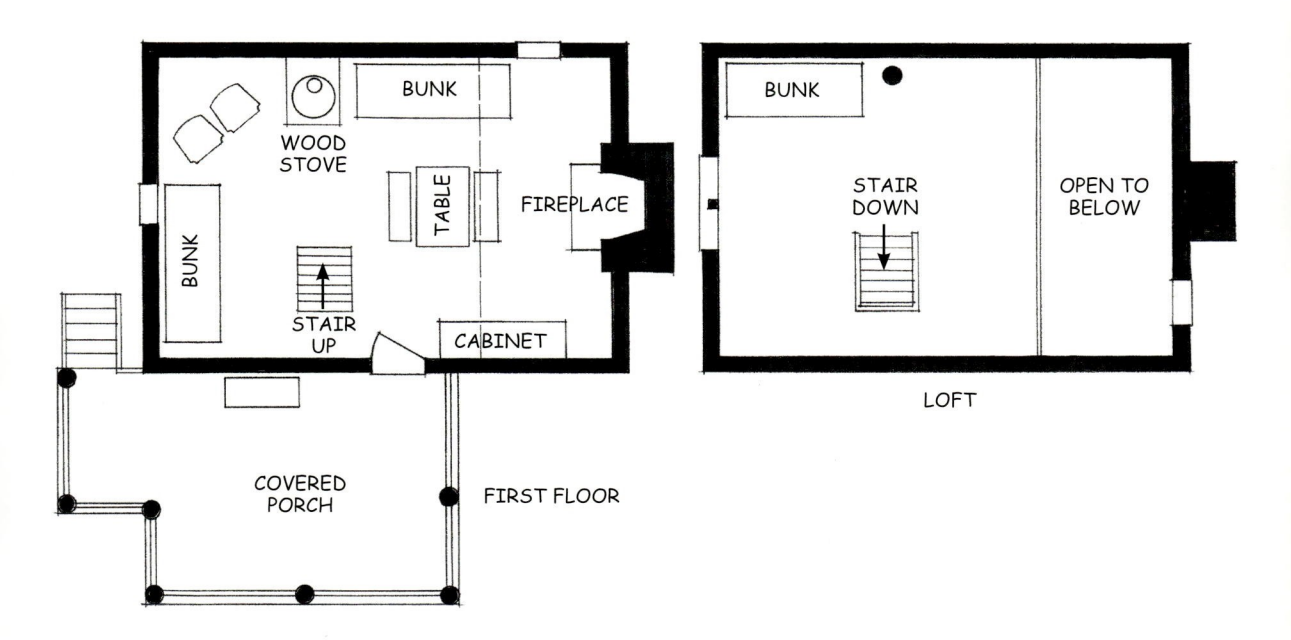

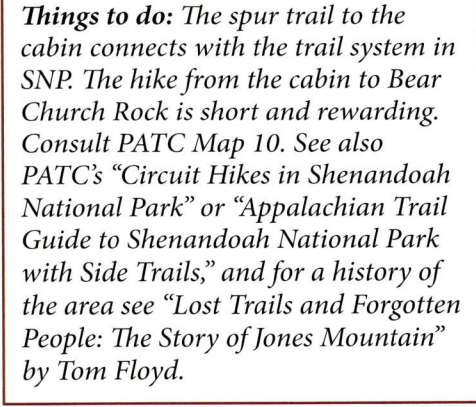

Things to do: The spur trail to the cabin connects with the trail system in SNP. The hike from the cabin to Bear Church Rock is short and rewarding. Consult PATC Map 10. See also PATC's "Circuit Hikes in Shenandoah National Park" or "Appalachian Trail Guide to Shenandoah National Park with Side Trails," and for a history of the area see "Lost Trails and Forgotten People: The Story of Jones Mountain" by Tom Floyd.

CABINS IN AND NEAR SHENANDOAH NATIONAL PARK, VIRGINIA

CABIN TYPE: Primitive

CAPACITY: 10

LOCATION: In Central District of SNP, 5.5 miles north of Swift Run Gap

MAP: PATC Map 10, 0.1 mile to AT by connector trail

BUNKS & BEDS: 3 double-width, double-deck bunks and 5 mattresses (bottom of one bunk is used for storage)

COOKING: Inside wood stove; outside fireplace on porch

HEAT: Wood stove

OUTSIDE FIRE: In fireplace only

WATER: Spring about 100 feet south of cabin (spring may be dry during drought conditions)

TOILET: Outhouse

ELECTRICITY: No

PETS: Allowed

Pocosin Cabin

Pocosin, pronounced poh-COH-sin, is an Indian name generally connoting a marsh, swamp, or tract of low land subject to flooding, but the word is used in soil science in southeastern Virginia for a relatively high, undrained flat area. Located in the southern part of the Central District of SNP, the Pocosin cabin looks eastward from a 3,117-foot elevation over a forested valley and the piedmont. Its name was taken from the Upper Pocosin Mission, which was founded by an Episcopal priest in 1904 but is now abandoned and in ruins.

    The cabin is a cozy one-room, square log structure, but big enough for ten people. The inside table seats six, while the outdoor picnic table seats eight. The cabin was built by the Civilian Conservation Corps as a shelter to house workers building Skyline Drive in the 1930s. It was later used by PATC members involved in building the AT. It presents a lovely view of a forested valley and the piedmont plateau and provides excellent hiking opportunities for both the novice and experienced hiker. With its short and easy hike-in, it is an ideal place for families with youngsters.

    Getting there: The cabin is 0.1 mile from the AT. Drive to the Pocosin Fire Road from Skyline Drive, either going south from Thornton Gap or north from Swift Run Gap. Though not specifically for the cabin, there is parking for up to eight cars about 250 feet in on the fire road. Do not block the fire road. If Skyline Drive is closed, the hike in is 2.1 miles from VA-642.

    Attention: Skyline Drive may close during snowfall, icy conditions, emergencies, and hunting season. Before leaving home, call SNP at 540-999-3500 regarding road closures. Be prepared to pay the Park entrance fee. During hunting season (mid-November to early January), the entrance gates close from 5:00 pm to 8:00 am.

DOUBLE-WIDTH BUNK (2) | TABLE | DOUBLE-WIDTH BUNK (2)

CUPBOARD

CUPBOARD

WOOD STOVE

DOUBLE-WIDTH BUNK (2)

TABLE

FIREPLACE

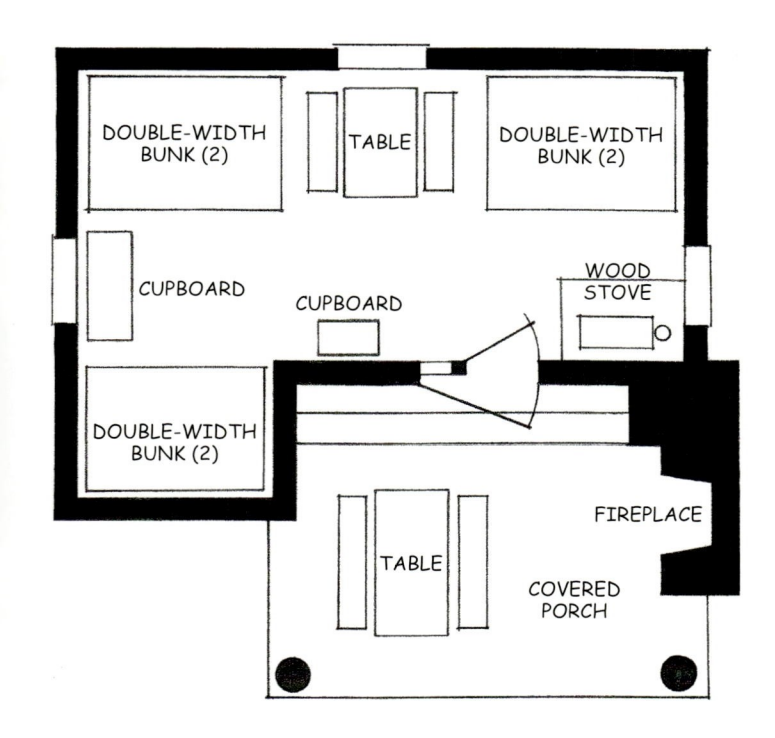

COVERED PORCH

Things to do: *Hike along South River Falls, Pocosin Mission, AT, and Bearfence Trail (great for sunset, reflected glow); also see activities listed for other SNP cabins.*

CABINS IN AND NEAR SHENANDOAH NATIONAL PARK, VIRGINIA

CABIN TYPE: Primitive

CAPACITY: 12

LOCATION: Adjacent to Central District of SNP in Pocosin Hollow

MAP: PATC Map 10; 3 miles to AT by trail

BUNKS & BEDS: 2 double beds, 2 bunks, and 6 folding cots

COOKING: Propane stove and wood stove, outside charcoal grill

HEAT: 2 fireplaces

OUTSIDE FIRE: In steel fire ring only

WATER: Water may be drawn from the stream

TOILET: Outhouse

ELECTRICITY: No

PETS: Yes

PATC Member-Only Cabin

Rosser Lamb Cabin

The Rosser Lamb farmhouse is a testament to the history of Appalachia and Shenandoah—the one before the park. The Lambs, one of the oldest families in Greene County, lived in the hollows around Pocosin Mission for over a hundred years. Hiram Lamb built this house in 1915, along with two others nearby. With donation of their Appalachian farmhouse, and over 100 acres by the Per-Lees (for whom the tract is named) to PATC, the Club is committed to keeping alive the heritage of the families who lived in the area before the park was created. The two individuals largely responsible for the renovations are Park Anderson and Peg Manuel. History comes alive on the tract. Renters can see what it was like to live in Appalachia 100 years ago.

   Getting there: Access is via state roads off of VA-230, with gravel/dirt roads for the last 3.1 miles. The final mile up the driveway is narrow and rutted. While four-wheel drive is not necessary, a higher clearance vehicle is best suited for this road. There is space for at least four cars in the parking area by the cabin.

   Attention: This cabin is not recommended for families with small children due to the very narrow and steep stairs to the second floor sleeping areas, which have no railings.

FIREPLACE
LIVING
TABLE
UP
HALL
PORCH

KITCHEN
WOOD STOVE
TABLE
LIVING
FIREPLACE
SCREENED PORCH
TABLE
TABLE
DECK

FIRST FLOOR

DOUBLE BED
BUNK
HALL
STORAGE
DOUBLE BED
BUNK

SECOND FLOOR

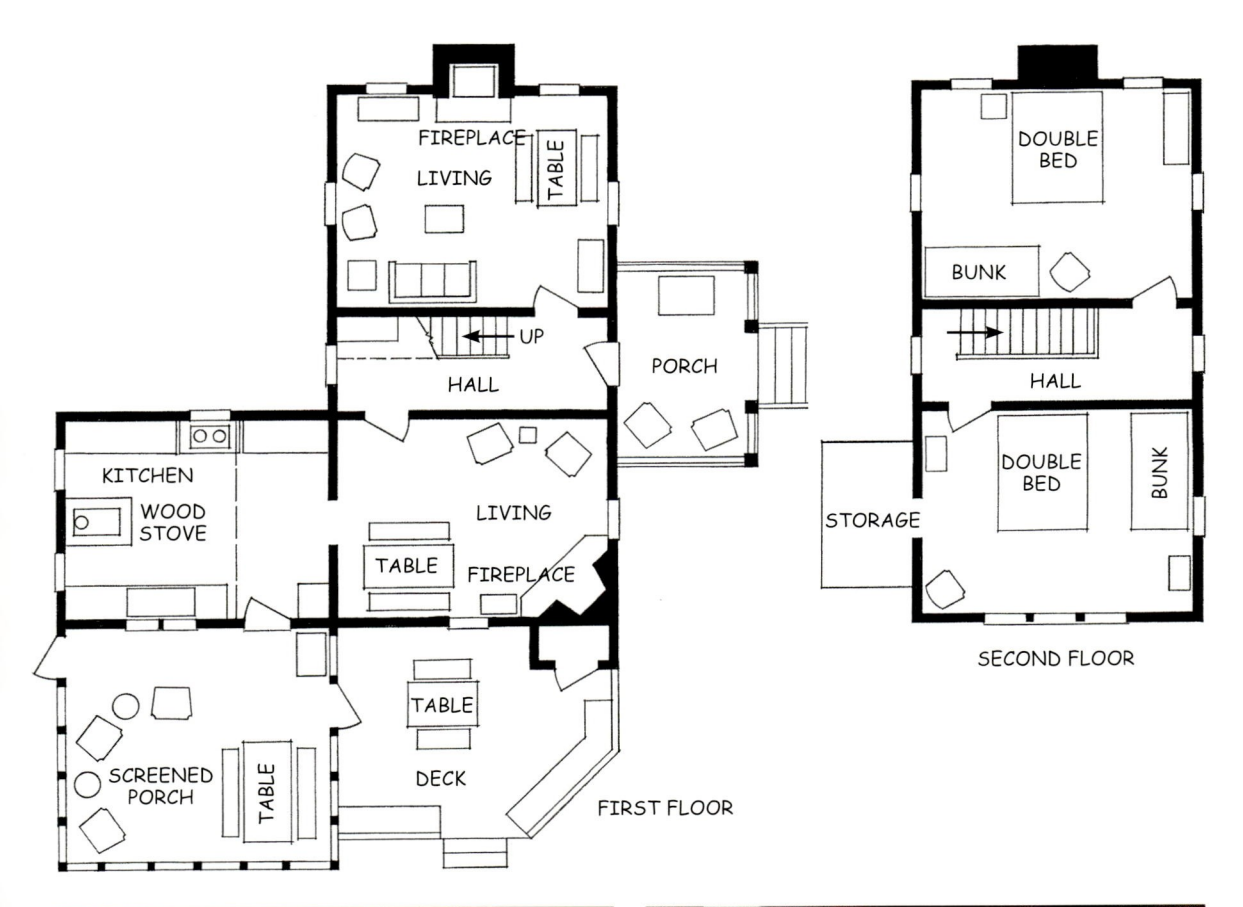

Things to do: Hike the Rosser Lamb to John's Rest Trail, which runs along Entry Run and used to be the old Mule Mail Road; a lovely stream and waterfall are nearby.

CABINS IN AND NEAR SHENANDOAH NATIONAL PARK, VIRGINIA

CABIN TYPE: Primitive

CAPACITY: 6

LOCATION: Near eastern side of the Central Section of SNP at end of Entry Run Road, north of Stanardsville, VA

MAP: PATC Map 10; 5 miles to AT by trail

BUNKS & BEDS: 1 double-deck bunk on first floor; space for 4 mattresses in loft

COOKING: Propane cooking stove and tank; outdoor charcoal grill

HEAT: Wood stove

OUTSIDE FIRE: In charcoal grill only

WATER: Spring is 300 feet downhill from cabin to right off trail

TOILET: Outhouse

ELECTRICITY: No

PETS: Yes

PATC Member-Only Cabin

John's Rest Cabin

John's Rest Cabin is a reconstructed rustic log cabin located near the beautiful Pocosin Mission site in Greene County, Virginia. In 1998 John Fischbach's family funded the reconstruction of the cabin on PATC property where John loved to hike and camp. The PATC property adjoins SNP to the north, and the Rapidan Wildlife Management Area to the west. A small river, Entry Run, is near the cabin giving the renter a great opportunity for fishing, exploring, or listening to the sound of rushing water.

The cabin has a main room, an upstairs loft, and a side porch overlooking Entry Run. It is located in a forest of mostly tulip trees. Flora include trillium, showy orchards, puttyroot, and ferns.

Getting there: VA-621 and VA-637, north of Stanardsville, lead to Entry Run Road, which goes to the gate and cabin parking area, where there is space for four cars. Hike-in is 0.4 mile beyond gate.

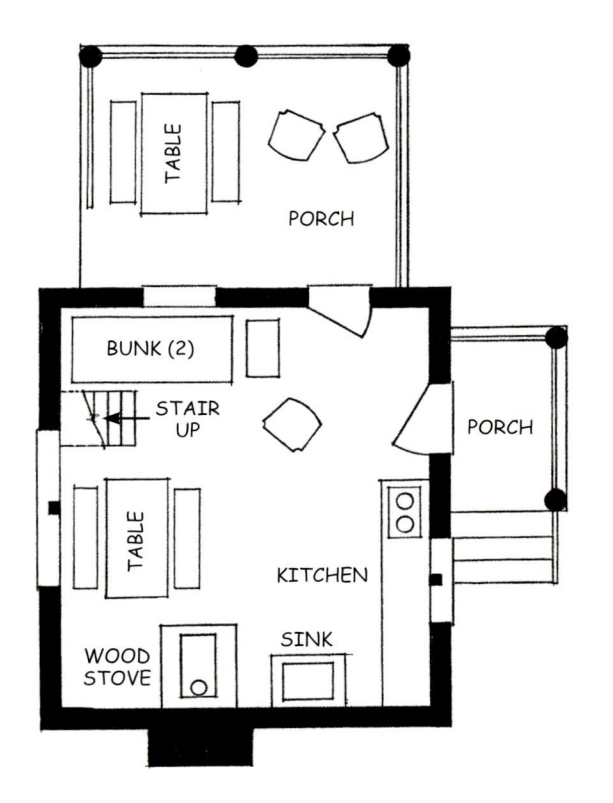

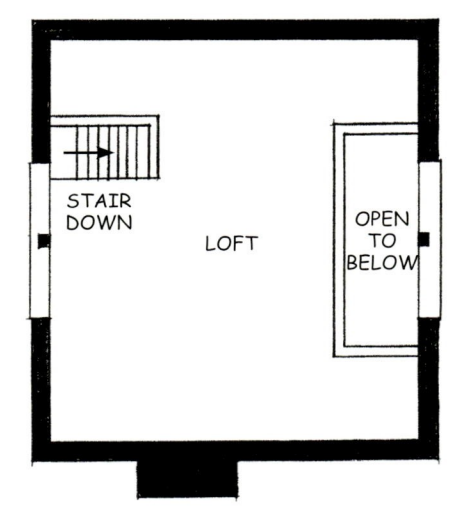

Things to do: *Do a nice loop hike from cabin on Entry Run Trail, or take trail into SNP (about 4 miles).*

CABINS IN AND NEAR SHENANDOAH NATIONAL PARK, VIRGINIA   **85**

CABIN TYPE: Primitive

CAPACITY: 8

LOCATION: In Southern District of SNP, west of Eaton Hollow Overlook on Skyline Drive, about 5.1 miles south of Swift Run Gap

MAP: PATC Map 11; 2.0 miles to AT from cabin via Skyline Drive; AT crosses drive just north of milepost 70 Powell Gap; there are no connecting trails from Argow cabin

BUNKS & BEDS: 4 double-deck bunks on second floor

COOKING: 3-burner propane gas stove for cooking; propane provided by PATC

HEAT: Wood stove and fireplace; fireplace alone will not heat cabin in winter

OUTSIDE FIRE: No

WATER: Small spring below cabin, but it may be dry during periods of draught

TOILET: Outhouse; outdoor solar shower available in warm weather

ELECTRICITY: No

PETS: Yes

PATC Member-Only Cabin

Argow Cabin

Argow Cabin is an 1850s chestnut log home formerly owned by Samuel Eaton (1828–1896). It is a two-story structure with a basement. The cabin sits on the 200-acre Firestone tract dedicated to Cliff Firestone, a long-time PATC member who left PATC his property and a sizable donation to help PATC purchase the Firestone tract, which borders SNP.

The acreage to the west is owned by Honorary Life Member Keith Argow. In keeping with the club's philosophy of preservation and conservation, Keith suggested that the club restore this historic chestnut log cabin located about 0.5 mile from the Schairer Trail Center and offered a generous donation to get the project started. After five years of weekend work trips, project manager Jeff Testerman and his crew of devoted and talented volunteers renovated the cabin. The cabin was dedicated to Mr. Argow on October 23, 2010.

Getting there: Drive south on Skyline Drive from the SNP's Swift Run Gap Entrance Station (US-33) for about for about 5.1 miles to the Eaton Hollow Overlook. Park near the southern end of the Overlook away from the view. Hike-in is 1.0 mile downhill. There is no access to the cabin from outside the Park to the west because coming in from that direction would cross private land.

Attention: Skyline Drive may close during snowfall, icy conditions, emergencies, and hunting season. Before leaving home, call SNP at 540-999-3500 regarding road closures. Be prepared to pay the Park entrance fee. During hunting season (mid-November to early January), the entrance gates close from 5:00 pm to 8:00 am.

SECOND FLOOR

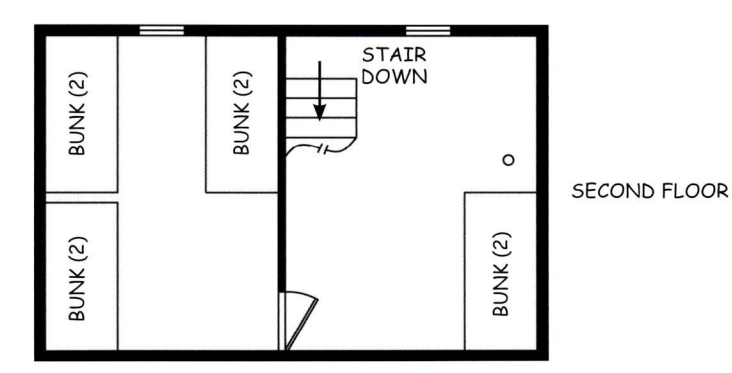

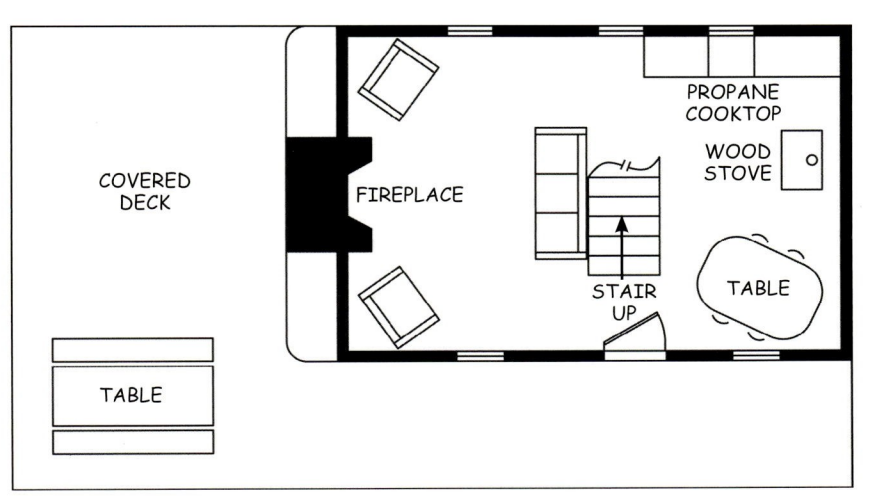

FIRST FLOOR

Things to do: *Hikes of varying lengths are possible. Using the roads above and below the cabin, a loop hike of about a mile can be made. The AT and blue-blazed trails in the Southern District of SNP can be accessed from Eaton Hollow Overlook, although getting to the AT requires walking almost a mile on Skyline Drive.*

CABINS IN AND NEAR SHENANDOAH NATIONAL PARK, VIRGINIA

CABIN TYPE: Semi-primitive

CAPACITY: 12

LOCATION: Off of Skyline Drive west of Eaton Hollow Overlook, SNP South District

MAP: PATC Map 11; 1 mile to AT by trail

BUNKS & BEDS: 4 bunks in front bedroom, 5 bunks in back bedroom, and 3 extra mattresses

COOKING: Gas stove

HEAT: Fireplace and wood stove

OUTSIDE FIRE: No

WATER: Running cold water in kitchen sink from May through October; in colder weather, water is from outside spigot; in severe conditions, water may be obtained from spring below cabin

TOILET: Outhouse (please conserve toilet wood chips and use only as needed)

ELECTRICITY: No, but there are propane lights inside cabin

PETS: Yes

PATC Member-Only Cabin

Schairer Trail Center

Named for J. Frank Schairer, one of the PATC founders and its first Supervisor of Trails, the trail center is situated on a ridge that provides spectacular views of Rocky Mount and the Massanutten Mountains to the west and Bush Mountain to the east. The Center sits on 200 acres of PATC land that was purchased by long-time PATC member Cliff Firestone to protect the western viewshed of SNP. A deck with several picnic tables extends along the west side of the building, providing views of the Shenandoah Valley and distant mountains.

Getting there: Take Skyline Drive south from the Swift Run Gap entrance (US-33) for about 5 miles to the Eaton Hollow Overlook, where there is parking for up to three cars. The hike-in from there is about 0.5 mile on a side-cut trail that can get icy in winter.

If Skyline Drive is closed, park your vehicle off the road near the Swift Run Gap entrance station and hike Skyline Drive for approximately 5 miles to the Eaton Hollow Overlook.

Attention: Skyline Drive may close during snowfall, icy conditions, emergencies, and hunting season. Before leaving home, call SNP at 540-999-3500 regarding road closures. Be prepared to pay the Park entrance fee. During hunting season (mid-November to early January), the entrance gates close from 5:00 pm to 8:00 am.

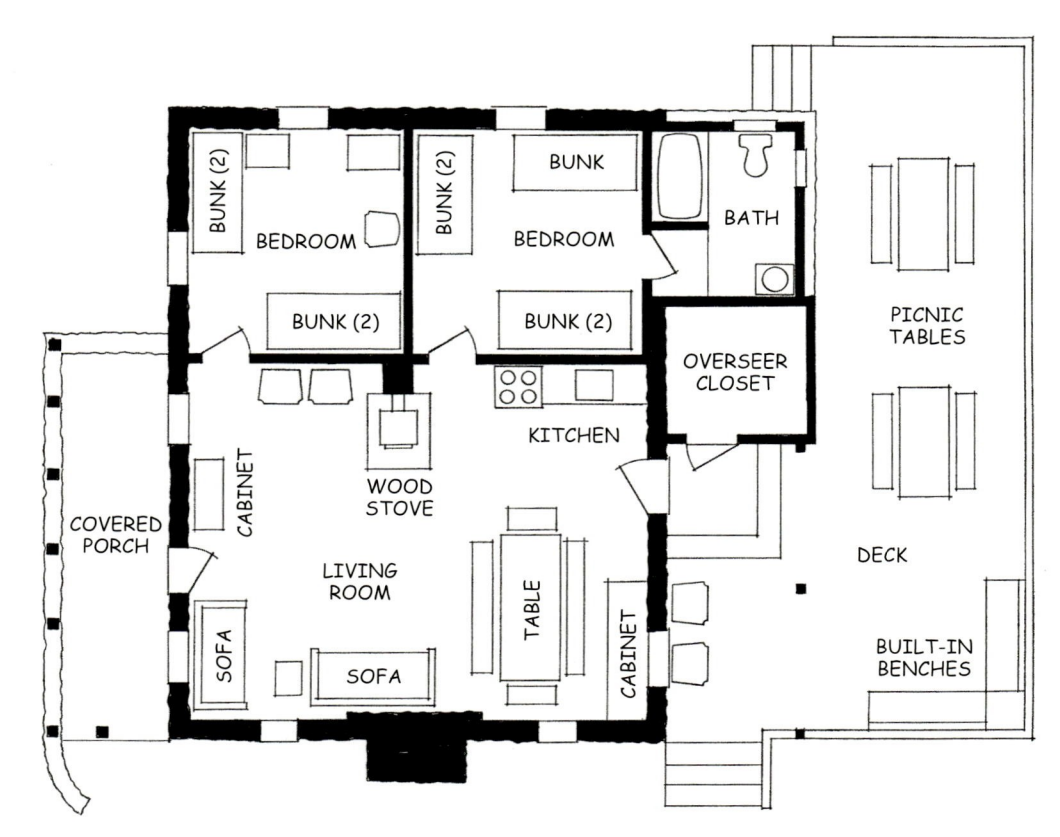

Things to do: Argow Cabin, an interesting old, hand-hewn chestnut log structure on the property, is thought to have been built by Samuel Eaton in the early 1800s. There are several circuit hiking trails in the area accessible from Skyline Drive. The AT can be accessed from Powell's Gap at milepost 70.

CABINS IN AND NEAR SHENANDOAH NATIONAL PARK, VIRGINIA

CABIN TYPE: Primitive

CAPACITY: 12

LOCATION: In South District of SNP, 0.6 mile west of Loft Mountain Campground

MAP: PATC Map 11; 0.3 mile to AT by connector trail

BUNKS & BEDS: 2 double-width, double-deck bunks and 2 double-deck bunks; mattresses for 12

COOKING: Wood stove

HEAT: Wood stove

OUTSIDE FIRE: In porch fireplace only

WATER: Reliable spring is 110 yards downhill from cabin, on Doyles River Trail

TOILET: Outhouse

ELECTRICITY: No

PETS: Yes

Doyles River Cabin

Doyles River Cabin lies in an exceptionally fine setting in the South District of SNP south of Swift Run Gap. From its elevation of about 2,800 feet, it overlooks a picturesque valley with views of Cedar Mountain and Via Gap. The sunsets, either from the porch, the huge rock in front of the cabin ("Pride Rock"), or Skyline Drive, are particularly striking. As night falls, deer, as well as foraging raccoons, can usually be seen. It is the favorite of many despite the heavy use of the Doyles River Falls Trail by summer vacationers in SNP and campers from the nearby Loft Mountain campground.

Architects of the National Park Service prepared the plans for this one-room cabin in June 1935. It was constructed in 1936 by artisans assisted by members of the Civilian Conservation Corps. The walls are of timbers sawed 10 inches square from seasoned chestnut logs, with the surfaces chipped to simulate rough dressing and with the four edges beveled.

Getting there: The cabin is off of Skyline Drive south of the Swift Run Gap Entrance station at US-33. From the Doyles River Overlook parking area, the hike-in is downhill for almost 0.5 mile, then uphill for about 100 yards.

When Skyline Drive is closed, the hike-in from VA-629 is 4.3 miles with an elevation gain of 1,700 feet and is for experienced backpackers only. VA-629 may be delayed in getting plowed free of snow.

Attention: Skyline Drive may close during snowfall, icy conditions, emergencies, and hunting season. Before leaving home, call SNP at 540-999-3500 regarding road closures. Be prepared to pay the Park entrance fee. During hunting season (mid-November to early January), the entrance gates close from 5:00 pm to 8:00 am. The steep drop in front of this cabin may be dangerous for young children.

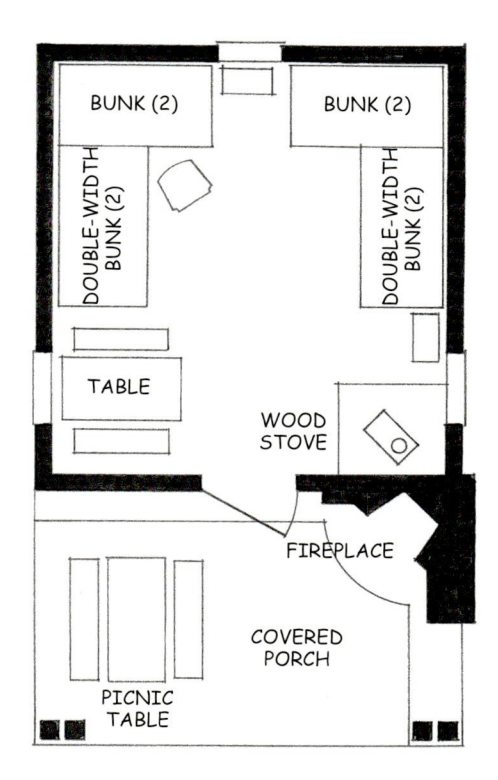

Things to do: Hike the AT or hike an 8 mile circuit via the Doyles River Trail, Jones Run Trail, and the AT. Hike the Big Run area or the Rockytop Trail.

CABINS IN AND NEAR SHENANDOAH NATIONAL PARK, VIRGINIA

CABIN TYPE: Primitive

CAPACITY: 9

LOCATION: Above Lydia, VA, on PATC's Vining Tract that borders the east side of SNP's Southern Section

MAP: PATC Map 11; no trail to AT

BUNKS & BEDS: 1 double-width, double-deck bunk; 5 bunks; loft and front deck benches provide additional sleeping options

COOKING: Wood-burning cook stove

HEAT: Wood-burning heating stove

OUTSIDE FIRE: Only in the stone fire ring in the meadow below the cabin

WATER: Closest spring 250 yards to west, often dry; most reliable spring is south of Morris Cabin, 440 yards downhill

TOILET: Outhouse

ELECTRICITY: No

PETS: Yes

PATC Member-Only Cabin

Mutton Top Cabin

Situated on an open meadow, Mutton Top Cabin has a panoramic view of the Virginia Piedmont. The original cabin was built in the 1960s by the Craddock family, who donated it to PATC in 1983. This cabin burned to the ground in early 1989. The current cabin was designed by architect and PATC member Roberto Peña and was built by Cabins Construction Crew volunteers and dedicated in 1992. Many of the logs were salvaged from PATC's Sexton Cabin, previously located in the George Washington National Forest. Sexton was dismantled when its location was declared a wilderness area, which requires the removal of man-made structures. The new cabin is a one-story structure with a sleeping loft, a large porch, and a covered barbeque/deck area. It sits in the footprint of the original cabin.

Mutton Top's immediate area covers a good portion of the south slope of High Top Mountain and adjoins the SNP's South District at a point above the cabin. A ruin of an older cabin is nearby as are the original stone fences. The cabin is located above the village of Lydia, Virginia, on PATC's "Vining Tract" property. See page 17 for information about the Vining Tract.

Getting there: After passing through Lydia the paved road changes to gravel. The gate and parking area for two to three cars are about 0.8 mile up this road. The hike-in is 0.45 mile from the gate. The road beyond the gate is extremely rough and it is highly recommended that only four-wheel drive vehicles continue past the gate. The gravel road to the gate is a steep and winding road that normally is passable, but can be difficult to climb if muddy or eroded by rain, and it can be dangerously icy in winter. If unable to drive up the road due to weather conditions, then parking in Lydia is necessary.

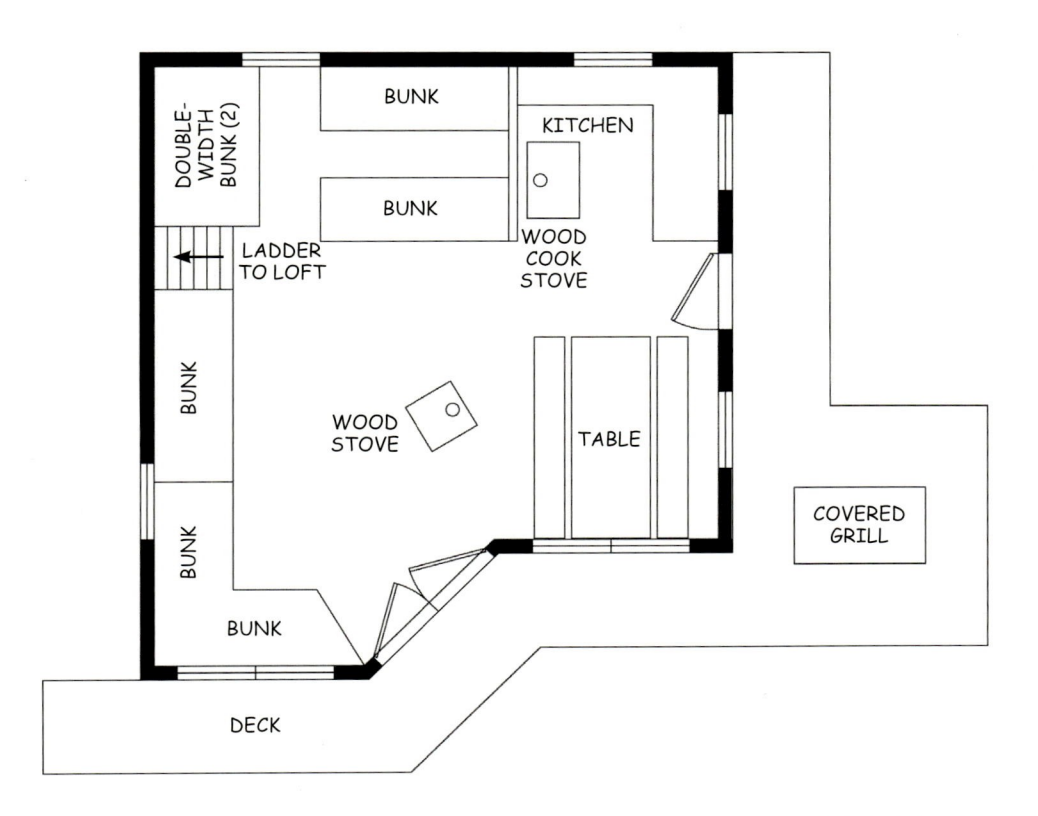

Things to do: Explore many old vestiges of Appalachian settlement on the Vining Tract including old orchards, fences, cemeteries, and building ruins; drive or hike to nearby SNP.

CABINS IN THE VINING TRACT, VIRGINIA   93

CABIN TYPE: Primitive

CAPACITY: 12

LOCATION: Above Lydia, VA, on PATC's Vining Tract that borders the east side of SNP's Southern Section

MAP: PATC Map 11; no trail to AT

BUNKS & BEDS: 12 mattresses; 3 bunks in living room, 1 double-width bunk in room off porch, 2 bunks and space for mattresses on loft floor

COOKING: Wood cook stove; outdoor cooking area

HEAT: Wood heat stove in living room and wood cook stove in kitchen

OUTSIDE FIRE: In outdoor cooking area only

WATER: Spring is 50 feet west and down the trail from kitchen

TOILET: Outhouse

ELECTRICITY: No

PETS: Yes

PATC Member-Only Cabin

Morris Cabin

Morris Cabin is named for Wayman Morris who started building in 1927 on land that had been his mother's. He grew corn on fields that were then open down to Conley Cabin, and raised horses on pasture land that extended uphill to the current location of Mutton Top Cabin. Morris Cabin is located above Lydia, Virginia, on the Vining Tract obtained by donation and purchase from Dr. and Mrs. Rutledge Vining. (See page 17 for information about the Vining Tract.)

The four-room cabin includes a kitchen/dining room, living room, bunk room, and upstairs loft. The cabin affords a view of the Virginia Piedmont in the distance. Beyond the back porch and past the privy runs an active and reliable spring that feeds into a cast-iron bathtub, which, according to legend, T. S. Eliot, W. H. Auden, Winston Churchill, and Bertrand Russell bathed in when it was located in a guesthouse at the University of Virginia.

Getting there: After passing through Lydia the paved road changes to gravel. The gate and parking area for two to three cars are about 0.8 mile up this road. The hike-in is about 0.5 mile from the gate. The road beyond the gate is extremely rough and it is highly recommended that only four-wheel drive vehicles continue past the gate. The gravel road to the gate is a steep and winding road that is normally passable, but can be difficult to climb if muddy or eroded by rain, and it can be dangerously icy in winter. If unable to drive up the road due to weather conditions, then parking in Lydia is necessary.

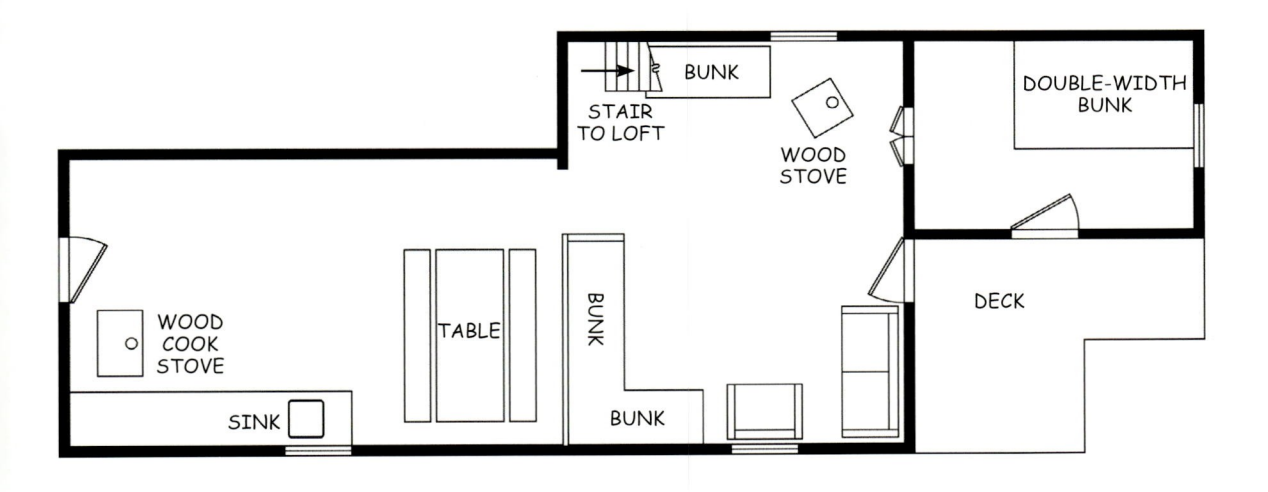

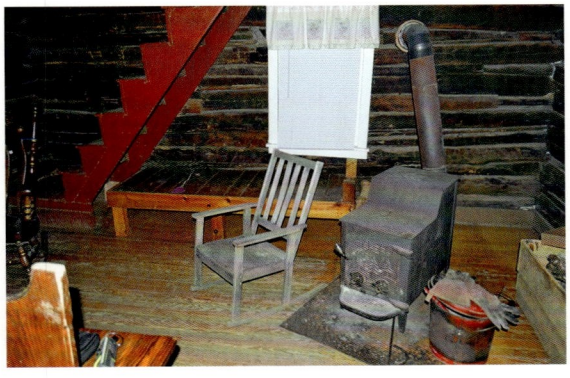

Things to do: Explore many old vestiges of Appalachian settlement on the Vining Tract including old orchards, fences, cemeteries, and building ruins; drive or hike to nearby SNP.

CABINS IN THE VINING TRACT, VIRGINIA 95

CABIN TYPE: Primitive

CAPACITY: 4

LOCATION: Above Lydia, VA, on PATC's Vining Tract that borders the east side of SNP's Southern Section

MAP: PATC Map 11; no trail to AT

BUNKS & BEDS: 1 double-width, double-deck bunk

COOKING: Wood stove for cooking and heating; outdoor grill in separate cook shed

HEAT: Wood stove for cooking and heating

OUTSIDE FIRE: In outdoor grill only

WATER: Spring is 0.3 mile away near Morris Cabin

TOILET: Outhouse

ELECTRICITY: No

PETS: Yes

Johnson Cabin

In 2003, PATC purchased the 70-acre Johnson property located along the western edge of the Vining Tract. (See page 17 for information about the Vining Tract.) The land had belonged to Louraine Morris, the mother of Wayman Morris after whom Morris Cabin is named. When Mrs. Morris died in 1953, Floyd and Ann Johnson purchased the land at a tax auction. The land eventually passed to their sons, Andrew and William. The Johnson brothers built the existing cabin in the early 1980s as a hunting cabin. The cabin is solidly constructed of logs salvaged from various outbuildings that had been part of the Morris farm. Surprisingly efficient use of the small 7 by 15 feet interior provides space for beds, a wood stove, table, chairs, and a Hoosier cabinet. A detached cookshed with counter space, a cooking grill, and a picnic table was added in 2005 for warm-weather cooking and lounging. Adjacent to the cabin is the house that belonged to Louraine Morris. Although the house is unfit for occupancy, it provides an example of how members of this mountain community lived in the first half of the 20th century.

   Getting there: After passing through Lydia the paved road changes to gravel. The gate and parking area for two to three cars are about 0.8 mile up this road. The hike-in is about 0.8 mile up the road from the gate. The gravel road to the gate is a steep and winding road that is normally passable, but can be difficult to climb if muddy or eroded by rain, and it can be dangerously icy in winter. If unable to drive up the road due to weather conditions, then parking in Lydia is necessary. The hike-in is 0.8 mile from the gate. The road beyond the gate is extremely rough and driving up to the cabin is not recommended.

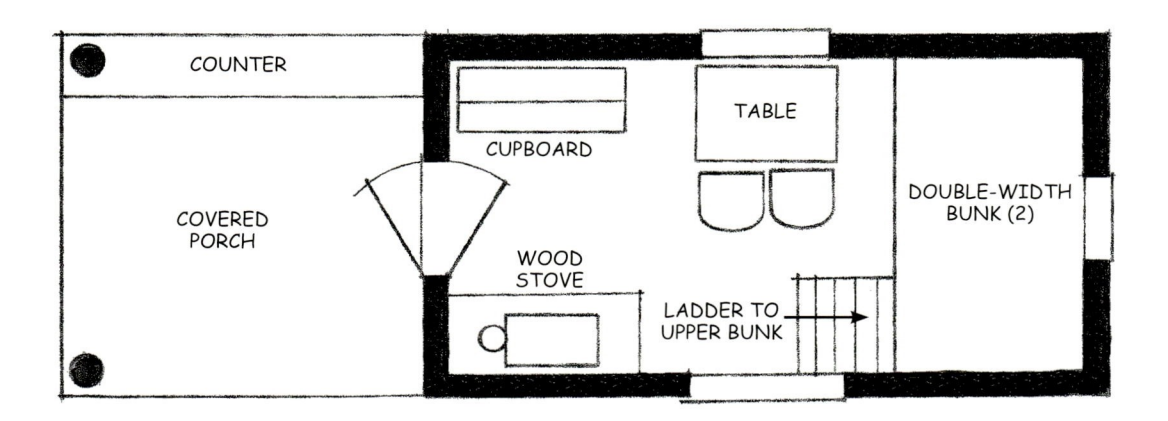

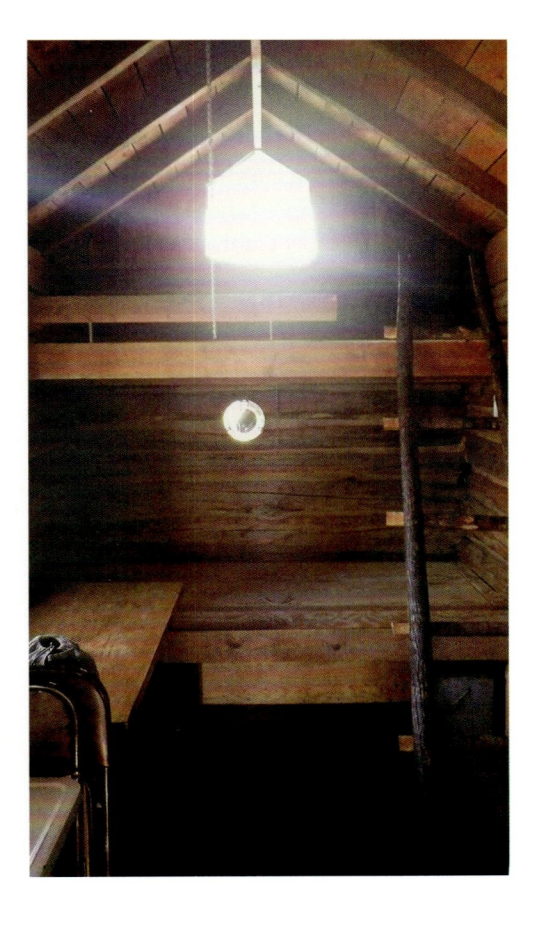

Things to do: Explore many old vestiges of Appalachian settlement on the Vining Tract including old orchards, fences, cemeteries, and building ruins; drive or hike to nearby SNP.

CABINS IN THE VINING TRACT, VIRGINIA

CABIN TYPE: Primitive

CAPACITY: 8

LOCATION: Above Lydia, VA, on PATC's Vining Tract that borders the east side of SNP's Southern Section

MAP: PATC Map 11; no trail to AT

BUNKS & BEDS: 1 double-width bunk on main floor; 2 bunks and floor space for 4 mattresses in loft

COOKING: Outside grill on covered deck

HEAT: Wood stove

OUTSIDE FIRE: No

WATER: Spring is 10 yards from cabin

TOILET: Outhouse; adjacent solar shower can be used in warmer weather

ELECTRICITY: No

PETS: Yes

PATC Member-Only Cabin

Wineberry Cabin

Lowest on the Vining Tract in elevation, but highest on the list of superbly reconstructed cabins is Wineberry. Dr. Vining believed that Elijah Conley lived here while constructing his own home, Conley Cabin, in the 1940s. (For information about the Vining Tract see page 17). The cabin was named after the wineberry vines that grow nearby, producing delicious berries in June and July.

Wineberry has imaginative touches that set it apart from the other cabins. Although small—14 by 20 feet—it boasts features guaranteed to amaze and amuse. The cabin is tin-roofed with a sleeping loft accessible via a hand-hewn mortise and tenon log staircase. The wood stove is hearty enough to have the cabin dubbed "Warmberry" on the coldest of winter nights. Outside are a roofed deck with a grill for cooking, an octagonal deck with matching picnic table, and a small rear deck for sleeping on warm nights. The cabin gets natural light from windows across the front of the loft, with stained glass panels made by one of the renovators. There is a solar heated shower by the outhouse, and, perhaps its greatest luxury, a clean and very reliable spring only a few feet from the cabin.

Getting there: After passing through Lydia the paved road changes to gravel. The gravel road to the gate is a steep and winding road that is normally passable, but can be difficult to climb if muddy or eroded by rain, and it can be dangerously icy in winter. If unable to drive up the road due to weather conditions, then parking in Lydia is necessary. The shared parking area for six cars and gate for the cabin are about 0.8 mile up this road. The hike-in is 0.5 mile from the gate, flat and then downhill on a woods road. Renters cannot drive past the gate to this cabin.

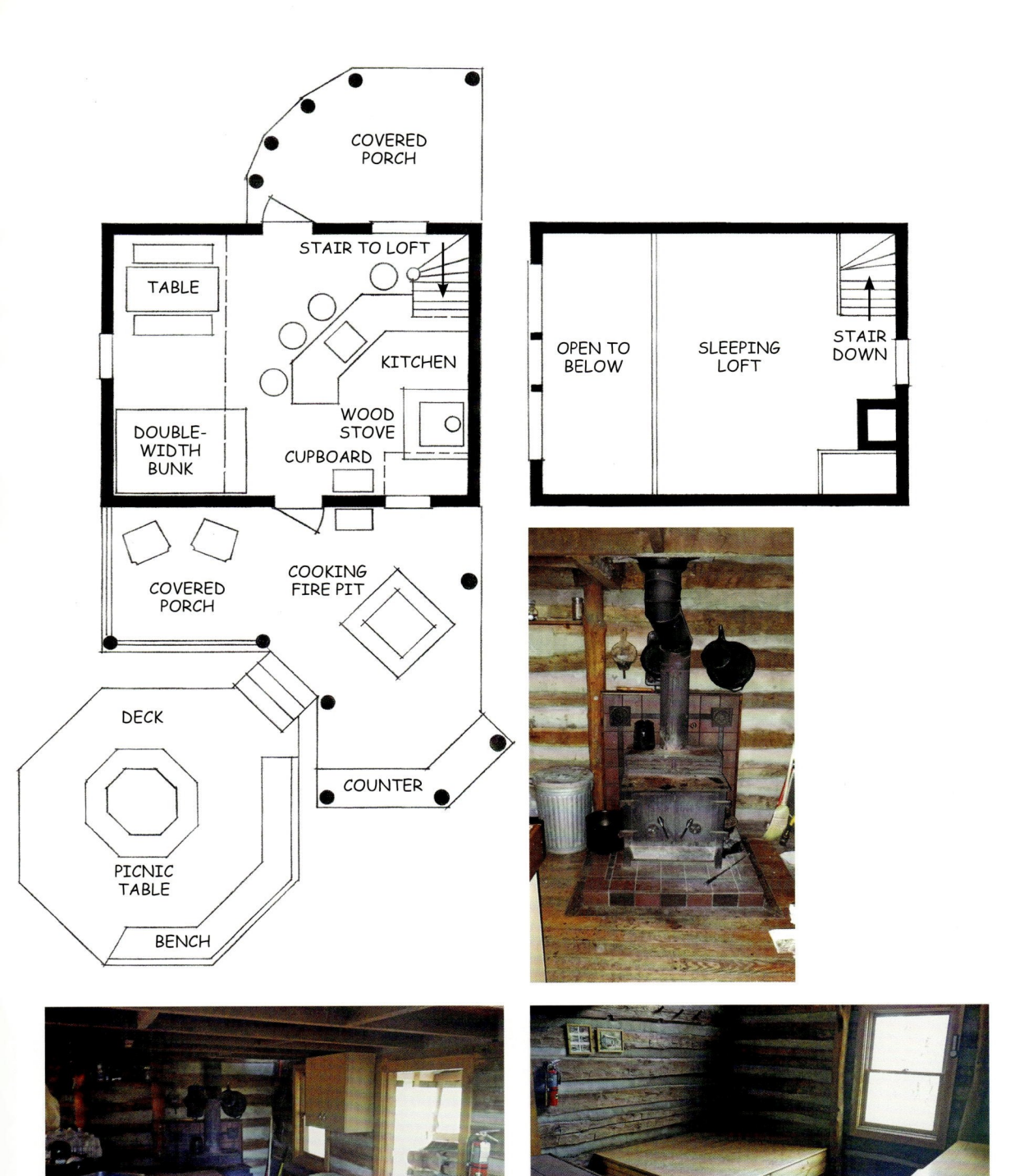

Things to do: *Explore many old vestiges of Appalachian settlement on the Vining Tract including old orchards, fences, cemeteries, and building ruins; drive or hike to nearby SNP. Take a hot shower in the solar shower or a cold plunge in the outdoor spring tub.*

CABINS IN THE VINING TRACT, VIRGINIA 99

CABIN TYPE: Primitive

CAPACITY: 8

LOCATION: Above Lydia, VA, on PATC's Vining Tract that borders the east side of SNP's Southern Section

MAP: PATC Map 11; no trail to AT

BUNKS & BEDS: 8 bunks with 8 mattresses

COOKING: Wood stove and covered outdoor grill

HEAT: Wood stove

OUTSIDE FIRE: No

WATER: Nearest spring is downhill on hike-in trail; a better but more distant spring is at Wineberry Cabin

TOILET: Outhouse

ELECTRICITY: No

PETS: Yes

PATC Member-Only Cabin

Conley Cabin

Conley Cabin was built by Elijah Conley in the 1940s. Originally sided with asphalt shingles, it has been resided with board and batten, and porches have been added on three sides. Adjoining the cabin is an outdoor cook shed with a stone grill. PATC completed renovations in 1994 and the cabin dedication was held in June 1995.

The south porch and open yard offer an exceptional view of the surrounding area. It is a large one-room cabin with a small cook stove and a recently added heating stove that heats the cabin well. The cabin is good for families because there is lots of open area for children to explore and still be visible. Just be aware of wildlife. There is also a tree swing.

The cabin is located above the village of Lydia, Virginia on PATC's "Vining Tract" property that borders the east side of SNP's southern section. (See page 17 for information about the Vining Tract.)

Getting there: After passing through Lydia the paved road changes to gravel. The gate for the cabin and parking area for about ten vehicles are about 0.8 mile up this road. The hike-in is 0.4 mile from the gate—you cannot drive past the gate to this cabin. The gravel road to the gate is a steep and winding road that is normally passable, but can be difficult to climb if muddy or eroded by rain, and it can be dangerously icy in winter. If unable to drive up the road due to weather conditions, then parking in Lydia is necessary.

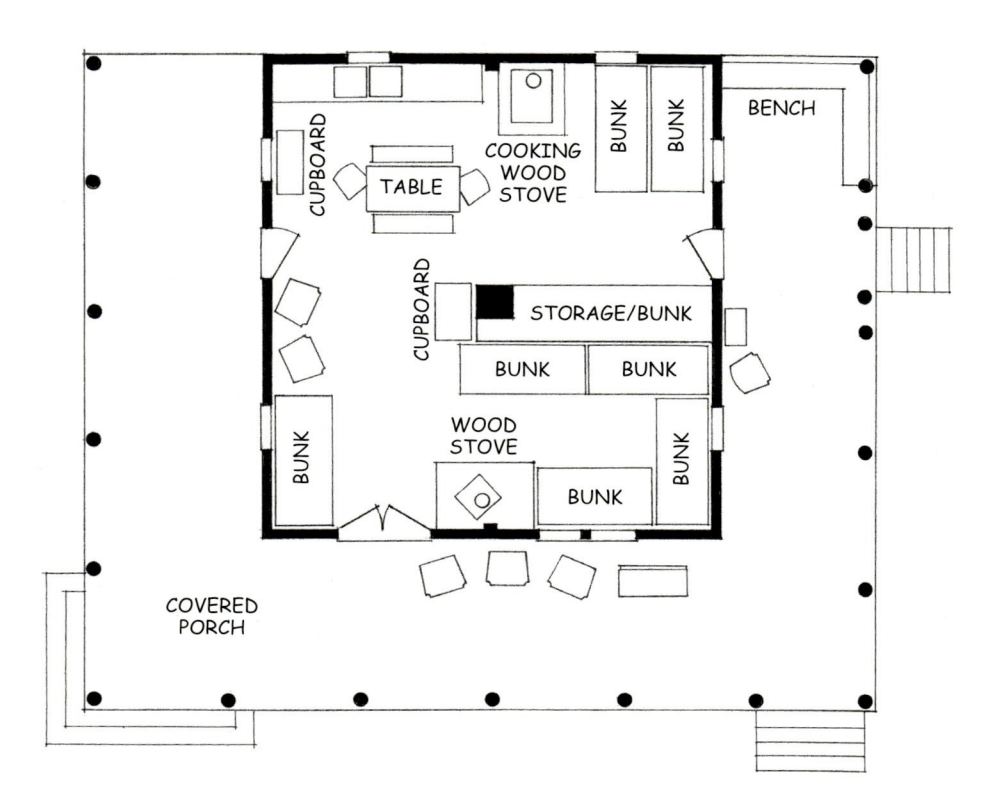

Things to do: *Explore many old vestiges of Appalachian settlement on the Vining Tract including old orchards, fences, cemeteries, and building ruins; drive or hike to nearby SNP.*

CABINS IN THE VINING TRACT, VIRGINIA **101**

CABIN TYPE: Modern

CAPACITY: 6

LOCATION: 4 mile northwest of Stanardsville, VA, on 675-acre Mutton Hollow Farm, adjacent to PATC's Vining Tract

MAP: PATC Map 11; no trail to AT

BUNKS & BEDS: 2 single beds; 2 fold-out futons

COOKING: Electric range with oven and broiler; microwave, refrigerator, and freezer

HEAT: 2 fireplaces

OUTSIDE FIRE: In charcoal grill only

WATER: Well water pumped to sinks and shower

TOILET: Indoor bathroom with sink, toilet, and shower on septic system

ELECTRICITY: Yes

PETS: No

PATC Member-Only Cabin

Vining Cabin

The Vining cabin is located on the 675-acre Daniel Vining family farm located in Greene County, Virginia. The cabin consists of the original chestnut log structure, estimated to be more than 100 years old, and a stone addition. The farm, leased to PATC by the Vining family, was previously owned by Daniel Vining's parents, Dr. and Mrs. Rutledge Vining. It is a classic example of a 19th century Appalachian farm containing a log cabin, numerous barns and other out buildings, and pastures surrounded by stone and split rail fences. Known as the Mutton Hollow Farm, it is located in a valley at the bases of High Top and Daniels Mountains and consists of extensive pasture land bisected by Mattie's Run. The farm is surrounded by rapidly rising forested hillsides that ascend nearly 1,000 feet to where the property adjoins PATC's Vining Tract, which was obtained by purchase and grant from the Vinings in the early 1980s.

Getting there: The cabin is 4 miles past Stanardsville, Virginia. The last 1.2 miles are on a gravel road that fords a small stream, then goes to the property's entrance gate. Parking for three cars is about 100 feet before the gate. The hike-in from the parking area is 0.4 mile.

Attention: While it is possible to drive up to the cabin with a good vehicle in good weather, great care should be used, especially in bad weather. There is room to park at least four more vehicles by the wood shed near the cabin.

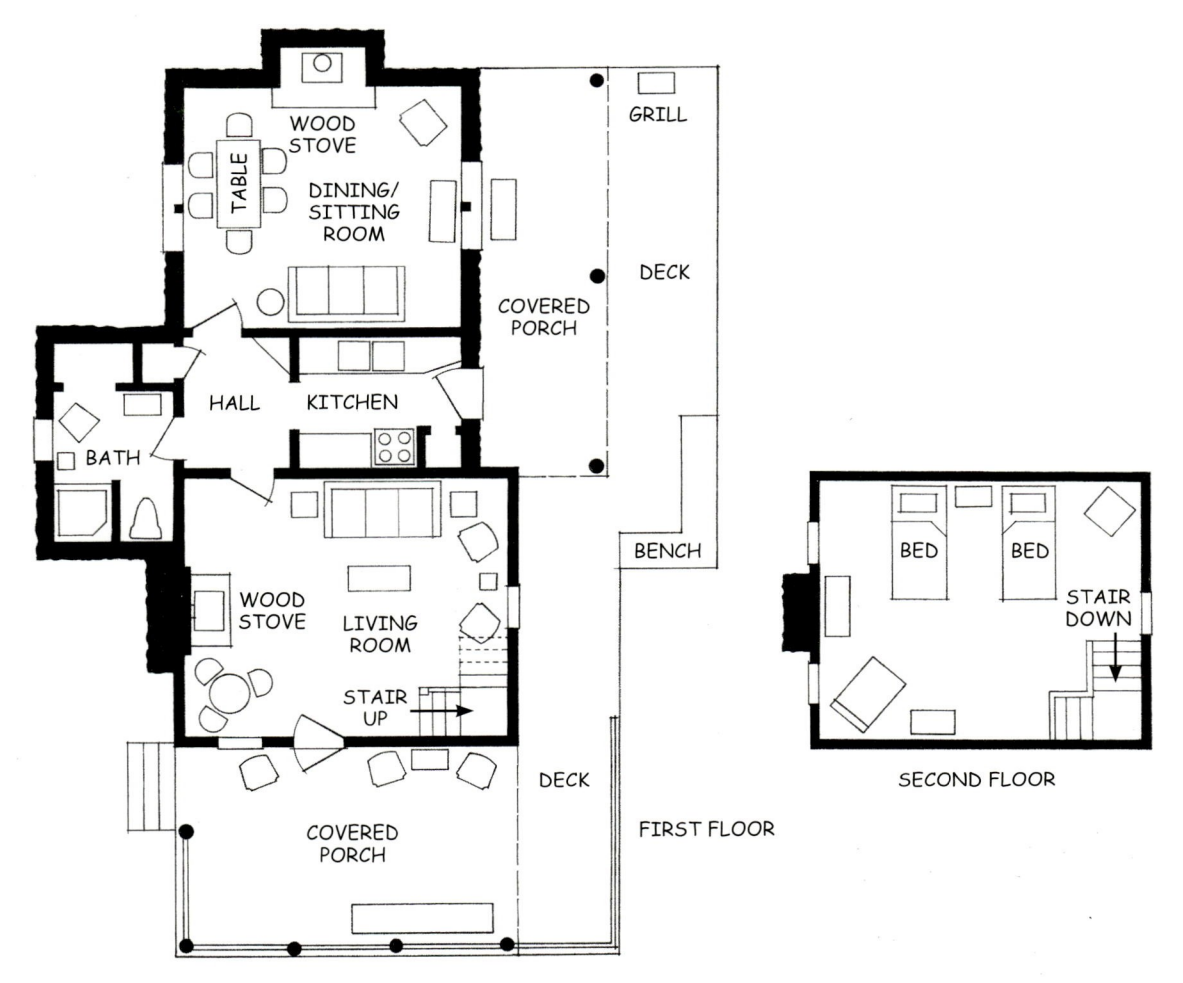

Things to do: Visit the various buildings on the farm and hike the roads and trails on the farm, including a trail to the PATC's Vining Tract.

CABINS IN THE VINING TRACT, VIRGINIA 103

CABIN TYPE: Modern

CAPACITY: 8

LOCATION: Charlottesville, VA, next to the University of Virginia

MAP: None; cabin is not close to AT

BUNKS & BEDS: 4 bedrooms, each with sleeping arrangements for two people (1 queen bed, 2 double beds, and 2 single beds)

COOKING: Electric oven and range, refrigerator, and dishwasher; outdoor barbeque pit

HEAT: Central air conditioning and oil heat; separate heat pump to run enclosed sun room; indoor fireplace

OUTSIDE FIRE: Patio garden fireplace

WATER: Hot and cold running water

TOILET: 2 bathrooms with sink, toilet, and shower; 1 bathroom with sink and toilet

ELECTRICITY: Yes

LAUNDRY: Washer and dryer in basement

PETS: No

PATC Member-Only Cabin

Dunlodge

The two Dunn brothers built Dunlodge in 1940. The house was built as a showplace of the type of construction the brothers could do, hence there are sections made up of logs, sloped roofs, step-down rooms, rose bud flooring, indoor fireplace, and wood beam ceilings.

Dunlodge is a four-bedroom, two and one-half bath house with central air conditioning and central oil heat, with a separate heat pump to run the enclosed sun room. The two-car garage is presently used as overseer storage and is not available to renters. There is a large outdoor slate patio with a rock fireplace. The five acres also includes a horse barn. A gated fence surrounds about one and one-half acres of the property where the main house sits.

Getting there: Dunlodge is within the city limits of Charlottesville, not far from the University of Virginia's Scott Stadium. There is parking by the cabin for about four cars.

> *Things to do:* A short hiking trail west of the cabin (see property map in cabin) connects to the University of Virginia Observatory Hill Trail system and the Rivanna Trail that circles Charlottesville for 19.5 miles. The cabin guest book further describes wineries, breweries, John Paul Jones Arena, UVA activities, historic places, and other things to do in the area.

SECOND FLOOR

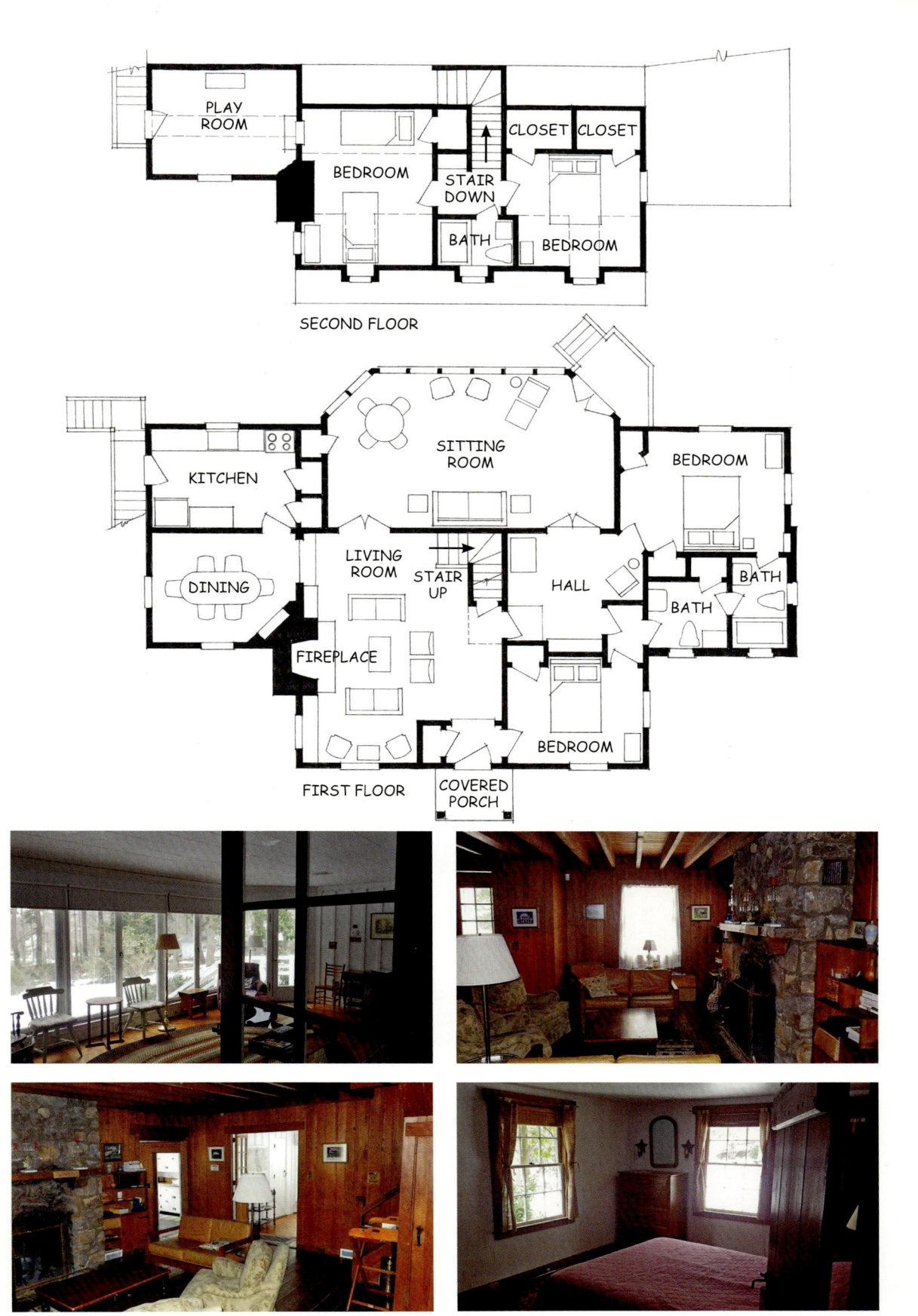

- PLAY ROOM
- BEDROOM
- STAIR DOWN
- CLOSET
- CLOSET
- BATH
- BEDROOM

FIRST FLOOR

- KITCHEN
- SITTING ROOM
- BEDROOM
- DINING
- LIVING ROOM
- STAIR UP
- HALL
- BATH
- BATH
- FIREPLACE
- BEDROOM
- COVERED PORCH

CABINS IN CHARLOTTESVILLE, VIRGINIA

Bears Den Lodge and Hostel

Bears Den Lodge and Hostel is owned and operated by the Appalachian Trail Conservancy. The historic stone mansion sits on 66 acres and is 150 yards from the AT and a beautiful, westward-facing overlook of the Shenandoah Valley and Blue Ridge Mountains. In addition to the rustic Bears Den Cottage that is managed by PATC (see page 48), Bears Den offers a drop-in, long-distance backpacker hostel with full services, accommodations for group or private party rentals, a primitive campground, and a contact for hiking, shuttle, and slackpack needs.

Built as a summer home in 1933, the Bears Den Lodge is reminiscent of a European castle and has been converted into a hostel. It is only 75 minutes from Washington, DC, and among the forested acreage are several lawns, trails, and quiet escapes. A main attraction is the famous Bears Den Rocks Overlook, which offers a stunning view of the Shenandoah Valley, especially at sunset.

All reservations are made directly with the Bears Den Office at info@bearsdencenter.org or phone 540-554-8708. Rates and more information can be found on the website at www.bearsdencenter.org.

Getting there: Bears Den is near Bluemont, Virginia (PATC Maps 7 and 8). Go 20 miles west of Leesburg off VA-7, turn left (south) at Snickers Gap onto VA-601 (Blue Ridge Mountain Road). The driveway entrance is 0.5 mile up the hill on the right.

PATC Cabins Summary

Cabin Name	Page No.	Cabin Location	Cabin Type	Pets	Capacity	PATC Map	Hike-in Distance	Distance to AT
PUBLIC CABINS								
Anna Michener	24	Pennsylvania	Primitive	Yes	14	2-3	1.0 mi	0.25 mi
Bear Spring	42	Maryland	Primitive	Yes	6	5-6	0.4 mi	0.8 mi
Bears Den Cottage	48	Virginia	Semi-Primitive	Yes	8	8	0.25 mi	300 ft
Catoctin Hollow Lodge	38	Maryland	Modern	No	8	5-6	0.75 mi	N/A
Corbin	66	SNP	Primitive	Yes	12	10	1.4 mi	1.5 mi
Dawson	34	Pennsylvania	Primitive	Yes	7	—	0.2 mi	N/A
Doyles River	90	SNP	Primitive	Yes	12	11	0.4 mi	0.3 mi
The Hermitage	32	Pennsylvania	Primitive	Yes	8	4	0.9 mi	0.7 mi
Johnson	96	Virginia	Primitive	Yes	4	11	0.8 mi	N/A
Jones Mountain	78	SNP	Primitive	Yes	10	10	3.8 mi	5.9 mi
Milesburn	26	Pennsylvania	Primitive	Yes	10	2-3	40 ft	60 ft
Olive Green	40	Maryland	Primitive	No	4	5-6	None	N/A
Pocosin	80	SNP	Primitive	Yes	8	10	0.2 mi	0.1 mi
Range View	58	SNP	Primitive	Yes	8	9	0.9 mi	0.1 mi
Rock Spring	70	SNP	Primitive	Yes	8	10	0.8 mi	0.2 mi
Sugar Knob	52	GWNF	Primitive	Yes	4	F	3.2 mi	N/A
MEMBER-ONLY CABINS								
Argow	86	Virginia	Primitive	Yes	8	11	1 mi	1.0 mi
Blackburn Trail Center	46	Virginia	Semi-Primitive	No	25	7	None	0.25 mi
Cliff's House	74	Virginia	Modern	Yes	6	10	None	N/A
Conley	100	Virginia	Primitive	Yes	8	11	0.4 mi	N/A
Dunlodge	104	Virginia	Modern	No	8	—	None	N/A
Glass House	54	Virginia	Modern	Yes	8	G	None	N/A
Gypsy Spring	28	Pennsylvania	Modern	Yes	6	2-3	None	1.2 mi
Highacre	44	West Virginia	Modern	No	8	7	None	30 ft
Horwitz	56	Virginia	Modern	No	6	9	None	4+ mi
Huntley	64	Virginia	Modern	No	6	10	None	2+ mi
John's Rest	84	Virginia	Primitive	Yes	6	10	0.34 mi	4.0 mi
Lambert	60	Virginia	Modern	Yes	8	10	0.1 mi	2.9 mi
Little Cove	30	Pennsylvania	Modern	Yes	8	K	None	N/A
Little Orleans	36	Maryland	Semi-Primitive	Yes	8	—	None	N/A
Meadows	72	Virginia	Semi-Primitive	Yes	12	10	0.2 mi	6.0 mi
Morris	94	Virginia	Primitive	Yes	12	11	0.5 mi	N/A
Mutton Top	92	Virginia	Primitive	Yes	9	11	0.45 mi	N/A
Myron Glaser	50	Virginia	Primitive	Yes	12	8	1.9 mi	0.2 mi
Old Rag	68	Virginia	Modern	Yes	8	10	None	4.0 mi
Robert Humphrey	76	Virginia	Semi-Primitive	Yes	8	10	None	N/A
Rosser Lamb	82	Virginia	Primitive	Yes	12	10	0.34 mi	3.0 mi
Schairer Trail Center	88	Virginia	Semi-Primitive	Yes	12	11	0.4 mi	1 mi
Silberman Trail Center	22	Pennsylvania	Primitive	Yes	8	K	None	N/A
Tulip Tree	62	Virginia	Primitive	Yes	8	10	0.1 mi	2.6 mi
Vining	102	Virginia	Modern	Yes	6	11	0.3 mi	N/A
Wineberry	98	Virginia	Primitive	Yes	8	11	0.39 mi	N/A

For current rental rates and polices see the PATC website: www.patc.net/cabins

ACKNOWLEDGEMENTS

Producing this book was a team effort. In addition to all of the volunteer PATC cabin overseers who reviewed the information about their respective cabins, the following volunteers and staff were responsible for the book's creation and production:

Editors
Anstr Davidson, Alan Kahan

Contributing Editors
Anne Corwith, Emeline Otey, Philip Paschall

Floor Plans and Photography
Bruce Berberick, Michael Hall, James Karn, Mel Merritt

Book Design and Production
Alan Kahan

Reviewers
Katherine Day, John Hedrick, Dick Hostelley, Mel Merritt, Kit Sheffield, Brewster Thackeray

Supervisor of Facilities
Mel Merritt

Located in the valley created by the Massanutten Mountains in the Shenandoah Valley of Virginia, Glass House is small, but well-equipped, and has a view of the east ridge of the Massanutten Mountains.